Women
Market Participation and Empowerment

Women
Market Participation and Empowerment

Seromena Asem

Foreword by
Professor Amar Yumnan

AKANSHA PUBLISHING HOUSE
NEW DELHI • GUWAHATI • VISAKHAPATNAM

AKANSHA PUBLISHING HOUSE
4649-B/21, Ansari Road
Daryaganj, New Delhi-110002
Phones: 23268193, 09435116718
Email: ektabooks@yahoo.com
visit us: www.akanshapublishinghouse.com

Women: Market Participation and Empowerment

First Published 2011

ISBN 978-81-8370-279-9

PRINTED IN INDIA

Published by Akansha Publishing House, New Delhi-110002 and printed at Harmain Offset Printers, Delhi.

Dedicated
to
My Beloved Parents

Contents

Foreword

Women studies have travelled a long way. In the beginning it was a kind of protest over the less than equal position of women vis-à-vis men. The move was spearheaded by radical workers for the cause of women and a very few understanding male. But it was mainly a limited move in the sense that the literature still encountered the problem of satisfactorily defining women. But the 80s and 90s of the last century significantly altered the dimension of the whole range of studies. From one oriented towards protesting against the prevailing scenario, the studies now started increasingly positive with increasing empirical appreciation of the actual position of women in a society and the developmental gains achievable through ameliorating that position. The foundations on equity and welfare considerations are very robust today than they were before.

Along with the global and national rise in the spread and density of women studies, there also followed such studies on the women of the North Eastern Region and for that matter of Manipur as well. These were in the beginning mainly contributions from women scholars from outside the region and who took interest in the manifest differential position of women in the region vis-à-vis their counterparts in the rest of the country. Slowly scholars from within the region followed suit. These studies were however manly verbose and qualitative.

The contribution of Dr. Seromena Asem's research lies in the fact that she endeavours to found all her analyses on the quantitative data she has collected herself. This at one go initiates a new trend of empirical orientation in women studies in Manipur. This in itself is a very laudable attempt. Further, she has done an extensive examination of the global scenario of women studies as well as the usual observations by the earlier contributions on studies about Manipuri women. In this way, she has been able to empirically re-examine the earlier statements of scholars working on women while at the same time opening new vistas for research.

This book is an interesting read.

Professor Amar Yumnam
Dean, School of Social Sciences
Manipur University

22 April 2011

Preface

To begin with, I can only express my gratitude to the Almighty, whose divine power helped me face the challenges in difficult times and guided me on the path of wisdom and success.

This book has grown out of the Ph.D. work I did in Manipur University. Whereas my basic academic training has been in the subject of Home Science, yet I had to undertake my research in the Department of Economics of the University in the absence of a formal department for pursuing research in Home Science.

At the 4th World Conference on Women held in Beijing in 1995 the United Nations declared that "poverty has a women's face" and that 70 per cent of the world's poor are women. Along with the usual consideration of income, the issues being raised related to lack of access to services and opportunities for human development, lack of a voice in political life and decision-making and social subordination and exclusion of women.

In this context, I choose to focus particularly on women of Manipur by studying the women vendors in the Khwairamband Keithel, the only well-known women market-place in Imphal. Women here have been historically, culturally and economically been active participants all along in the marketing process of the land. In fact, this market-place is one of the most important institutions of social change and centers to disseminate new ideas and spread civilization. This institutional and historical strength has been sustained through the millennia of society's evolution in Manipur.

The research work is carried out in order to fill up some of the gaps to the already existing literature of women studies in general and their specific problems in particular with insights from the Manipur experience.

The book consists of five chapters. The first chapter begins with an introduction to the subject of research pursued with a simple theoretical framework highlighting the links between gender equality and growth and poverty reduction. This was followed by an overview of relevant literature that has examined women's empowerment as the outcome of interest as well as an influencing agent on other development outcomes. It also gives the detailed structure of Sanakeithel (Khwairamband Keithel).

The second chapter gives a general picture on the relative status and position of women of Manipur right from the pre-colonial (before 1891) period to till date. This is done by using the available demographic indicators. To better understand women's status and position, it also concentrates on the role the women played in the socio-politico-economic process of the land.

Chapter 3 concentrates on a brief conceptual exposition of the market, followed by a picture of the location, origin and the present socioeconomic characteristics of the vendors in the Khwairamband Keithel.

Chapter 4 deals with on the push and pull factors of women for joining the labour market. For better understanding, we compare across the demographic variables such as age, type of family, education, size of family, marital status and number of earners. It also deals with how the large scale economic participation as well as the contribution of women in Manipur translates into actual empowerment outcomes by examining the five elements of empowerment, viz., economic contribution, economic independence, participation and autonomy in decision-making at household level, participation in the political activities and relevant and contemporary areas.

The last chapter, Chapter 5, provides a summary of the main findings and identifies some areas for further research.

Words can hardly express my deep sense of profound gratitude and indebtedness to my supervisor Prof. Amar Yumnam, who had made light of my work. His mastery of knowledge and spirited dedication to work throughout my long years of association has been a source of inspiration to me. Without his scolarly guidance, wise and painstaking advice, constant supervision and deep interest, my dream of this book wouldn't have been a reality.

I owe a special debt of gratitude to Dr. Laishram Suresh Singh for paving the path to this research work and providing me relevant articles and journals.

I acknowledge the excellent contribution and consultation provided by Maniton, Ethno Heritage Council (HERICOUN), Karam Manimohon Meetei, geographer, Manipur Census Office and N. Indramani Singh of Manipur State Archives, Government of Manipur.

I am also thankful to Chinglen Maisnam, Assistant Professor, Department of Economics, Manipur University for his timely help and support.

The assistance of my younger sister Ilu (Sujata), Pakpi and her brother during my fieldwork is greatly appreciated.

Thanks are due to my friend Ch. Nungshitombi Devi for her advice and significant support.

I owe special thanks to Eche Pem, Librarian, Manipur State Archives for her assistance in providing me the necessary documents and materials.

During my research work I have depended on various sources like books, journals, documents which I got it from National Library, Kolkata, Manipur University Library, Manipur Central Library, Institute of Cooperative Management, Manipur and Centre for Manipur Studies, Manipur University. The cooperation received from the staff members of all these libraries is gratefully acknowledged.

My especial gratefulness goes to women vendors of Khwairamband Keithel whose ready sharing of information and willing supply of personal data form the data foundation of this piece of research. Indeed it is only their willing cooperation that made my research work largely possible.

My utmost gratitude and heartfelt thanks to all my family members who endow me with their best blessings in the shape of power and ability, enabling me to give a final touch to my work in the face of various vicissitudes of life.

At length, I shall remain indebted to all the benevolent.

Author

List of Tables

List of Figures

1

Introduction

"Poverty has a women's face", and that 70 per cent of the world's poor are female.[1] The 'bottom line' measure of poverty in the above statement is lack of income, but it also consists of lack of access to services and opportunities for human development, lack of a voice in political life and decision-making, and social subordination and exclusion.[2]

We choose to focus particularly on women, because in every society they struggle against gender norms that limit their resources and opportunities for improvement, and because we know that women's empowerment is a tremendous resource for social change and a prerequisite in the broader fight against global poverty.[3]

Recent decades have witnessed an increase in women's participation in the labour market and erosion of the wage gender gap in most countries.[4]

A significant progress has been achieved in some areas after the creation of the United Nations Commission on the Status of Women in 1946, notably with regard to women's participation in the labourforce, a narrowing of the wage gap between men and women in some countries and an improvement in the level of education of women. However, in the majority of countries in the world, women are still at a disadvantage in terms of their role and position in the economy as compared with men (ILO, 2004). Despite the recognition of gender equality as a legitimate goal for humanity at large, gender inequality and discrimination against women still persist in the workplace. There are several reasons for this situation. In many societies, cultural, religious, or family norms continue to confine women to certain roles, and serve as barriers to their participation in economic life on an equal basis with men.[5] Furthermore, women are primarily responsible for the reproductive functions within the family, and for providing care to children and the elderly. These results in a division of labour within the household, which makes it difficult for women to take full-time jobs in the labour market. Even if women were able to participate fully in the labour market, discrimination against them might persist, despite its being economically inefficient, because the prevailing gender order gives more authority to men in society. And in order to preserve their authority, men would tend to exclude women from their decision-making networks.[6] Another explanation is related to the lack of information that employers may have about their women employees, resulting in their tending to underestimate the productive potential of women, and, therefore, paying them less and confining them to lower grade occupations.

These factors contribute to weakening women's capacity to earn their own income, especially as they render it difficult for women to access resources (such as land and credit) and other basic services (such as education and health care). Given their inferior role in society, their bargaining power in the workplace is also weak; the more so as they lack experience in organizing themselves as a negotiating or lobbying group. The outcome, in terms of the role and status of women in the economy, is reflected in insufficient participation in the formal labour market, poor conditions of work and quality of employment, job segregation (occupational stereotypes), lack of empowerment, and wage inequality for the same job as men.

Amartya Sen makes a compelling case for the notion that societies need to see women less as passive recipients of help, and more as dynamic promoters of social transformation, a view strongly buttressed by a body of evidence suggesting that the education, employment and ownership rights of women have a powerful influence on their ability to control their environment and contribute to economic development.[7]

Ample evidence suggests that greater gender equality in resources such as education and access to employment can reduce the likelihood of a household being poor. Female labour force participation, in particular, has been shown to play a key role in cushioning households from the impact of macroeconomic shocks and keeping households from falling into poverty.[8] Therefore, employment for women seems to be important not only because of the direct contribution it makes to household welfare, but because of the personal power it provides for women in shaping and making family decisions and in establishing social ties and networks beyond family.

So, women's equality is an absolute necessity if the blight of poverty is to be removed and the nations of the world are to create a secure, sustainable and prosperous future.[9]

As per the World's Woman, *Statistical Book on Woman,* UNO, New York (1955) woman is one-half of the total world's population, performs 2/3rd of the world's work and market over 3/5 of the world's food. Moreover, woman represents 3/5 of the world's total literates and occupies 1/10 of the world's income and less than 1/100th of the world's property. In the national scenario, out of the total 397 million workers, 123.9 million are women. Of these, roughly 106 million women work in rural areas and the remaining 18 million work in urban areas. Ninety six per cent of the women workers are in the unorganised sector. Overall the female work participation rate has increased from 19.7 per cent in 1981 to 25.7 per cent in 2001. In the rural areas, it has increased from 23.1 per cent to 31 per cent and in the urban areas from 8.3 per cent to 11.6 per cent. So, men receive the lion's share of income and recognition for their economic contribution- while most of women's work remains unpaid, unrecognized and undervalued.

Unrecognizing and undervaluing women's work has an impact on the status of women in society, their opportunity in public life and the gender- blindness of development policy.[10]

Nehru emphatically wrote "If you want me to tell you what a nation is like ,or what a social organization is like, tell me the position of women in that country".[11]

Now, with the turn of century women's role is increasingly recognized that in economic development, the growth pattern should subserve the goal of distributive justice. After the women conference in Nairobi in 1988, women researchers and activists fighting for recognition and participation in the planning process understood that economic justice remains central to any improvement in the status of women in the Third World.[12]

Theoretical Considerations

In mainstream economics there is a long tradition of neglecting female contributions to societal well-being. Already with Adam Smith's work "*The Wealth of Nations,*" goods that were not traded over markets but remained within the realm of the single household used not to belong to the subject matter of economic analysis.[13] But, traditionally, it is those goods that are created and consumed within the "identical household" that are produced by its female members. Only when women started producing for strangers, or when the share of women in permanent employment outside the household rose, did female work and female pay become part of economic investigation.[14] Formal theoretical treatments of gender equality, particularly of their effects on well-being, nevertheless remain rare in the economics literature. In the following, we outline a simple theoretical framework highlighting the links between gender equality and women empowerment and its positive outcome.

Figure 1 shows, *increases in female earnings* can, on the one hand, reduce current poverty and stimulate short-term growth through higher consumption expenditures, and, on the other hand, reduce future poverty and stimulate long-term growth through higher savings.[15]

To the extent that increased female earnings leads to higher bargaining power for the woman in the household, increased earnings has an indirect effect of promoting increased child well-being.

Children's wellbeing is another pathway through which increased gender equality may be associated with poverty reduction and growth (see Figure 1). Increases in maternal education and control over household resource allocation improve child wellbeing, educational attainment and health. This, in turn, leads to increases in children's cognitive ability and productivity as adults (Hoddinott et al. 2005; Behrman and Alderman, 2006). Thus, increases in women's influence over decision-making in the household leads to an intergenerational transmission of earnings capability and this, in turn, improves prospects for poverty reduction and growth in the future.

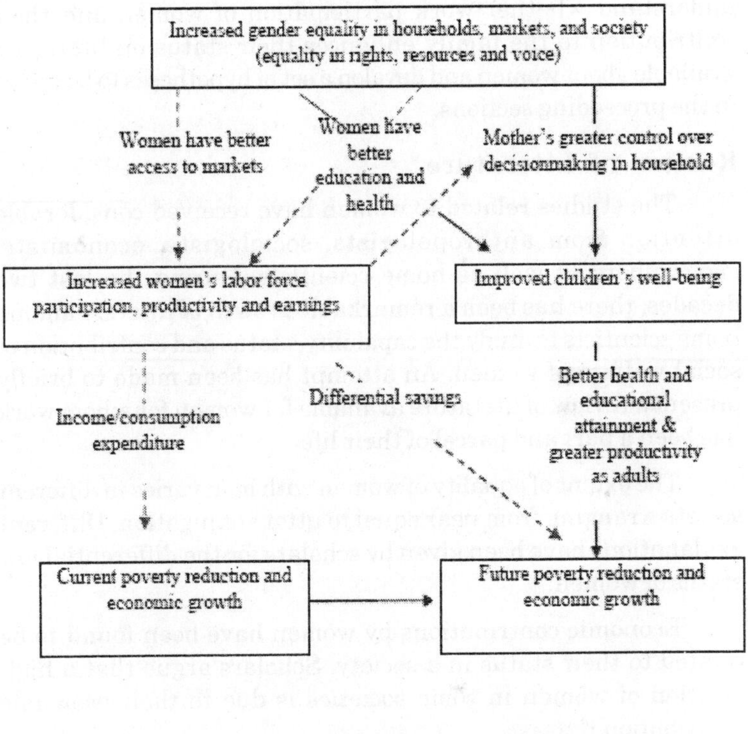

Figure 1. A framework for understanding the links between equality and growth/poverty reduction

Note: This above framework is reproduced from Andrew Morrison, Dhushyanth Raju, Nishtha Sinha, (2007)-*Gender Equality, Poverty and Economic Growth*—a product of the Gender and Development Group, Poverty Reduction and Economic Management Network. This framework helps us focus development interventions, as well as provide guidance for monitoring empowerment processes and outcomes.

Thus, gender balances and equalities should be viewed as a process towards alleviating poverty and thereby providing the opportunity for women to be considered as equal partners in improving well-being. Therefore, an effort is generate to better understand whether work participation of women and their contribution to the family enhances their status on literature available about women and develop a set of hypotheses to be tested in the proceeding sections.

Review of Literature

The studies related to women have received considerable attention from anthropologists, sociologists, economists, geographers as well as home scientists. During the last two decades, there has been a remarkable growth of interest among home scientists to study the capability, status and contribution to social welfare of women. An attempt has been made to briefly present a review of literature available for women for whom work has been a part and parcel of their life.

The extent of equality of women with men varies in different societies ranging from near equal to utter subjugation. Different explanations have been given by scholars for the differential low status of women.

Economic contributions by women have been found to be related to their status in a society. Scholars argue that a high position of women in some societies is due to their economic contribution.[16]

Contrary to the above argument, other scholars have argued that economic contribution by itself is not enough for women to have an equal status. They must have control over the means of production and should have opportunities for equal participation in family and community decision-making.[17] These two perspectives become very clear if we look at the results of different studies, which have shown varying results on women and work.

One of the most important findings for women entering the job market is economic consideration, whether out of a dire necessity or for supplementing the family income for attaining/ maintaining higher standard of life.

It has been found in many of these studies Kapur (1970), Ramanamma (1979), Ranade (1970), Krishna Raj ((1978), Hate (1969), Mies (1980) that respondents had to support their families. Ross mentioned "Indeed the main reason that so many married Hindu middle class women work without reproach is because everyone understands the economic problem of the middle class and that a wife's income is often essential to the family's standard of living". This has been supported by the findings of the Committee on Status of Women as mentioned in the report, "Rising prices and levels of unemployment, added to the increasing costs of education and housing and absence of social security have increased the degree of economic pressures on the major section of the class."

A report, "Women, Wife and Worker" (1960) published by Social Science Department of the London School of Economics, reported about the position of women at Mesrs. Peck Freon Limited— a biscuit manufacturing concern which was predominantly staffed by women workers. The report concluded: "From what the women themselves said, there was no doubt that they worked mainly for financial reasons". For the women whose husbands were in regular employment, it was not for the sheer necessities of life that more money was required. For these women the aim was for a higher standard of living for their families.

Contrary to the popular belief that women's interests in employment are transitional or temporary, the indications from the Tata Institute of Social Sciences, Bombay (1962) and Delhi School of Social Work (1962) surveys conducted by the National Council of Women's Education, India are that most of the respondents were interested in their jobs or liked to work, as far as their circumstances permitted, because the working condition were generally good. The second important reason for the job liking was as a source of income. Some had a liking for the job, because it helped to increase their knowledge or because it helped them in getting good social contacts or even because employment helped them to be busy.

For married women who work, the public sphere of job and the private sphere of home and family are seldom maintained as separate and distinct as they can be for many men. Obviously, both men and women have responsibilities on each of these spheres.

Men can usually divide up their time and their commitment devoting home and work, but for women these areas of responsibilities and the exceptions from them cannot be so readily compartmentalised. This has resulted in much discussion about the women's two roles[18] and about the problem combining, the dual responsibilities.[19] These difficulties become particularly acute when there are children in the family. Regarding child care and women's employment Basu and Basu (1991), Bianchi, S., (2000), concluded that women's familial roles and their market activities diminishes the time available for child care which in turn results in poor health outcomes and higher mortality for children. Contrary to the above findings Khandker and Latif (1996) note that increasing employment and income earning opportunities especially for women is the only short-run measures for curtailing both infant mortality and fertility and will help in improving children's well-being.

While there have been some who feel that economic participation does not immediately lead to share in authority structure, there are others who definitely believe that economic participation, besides extending her role and exposing her to outside forces, also qualitatively changes her own perception and lends her self-confidence.

Sathar and Kazi (1997), Mukhopadhyay (1999), claimed that earning an independent income lead to an increase in women's ability to exercise 'voice' in the household decision-making process. It further concluded that women who generated income have gained respect and greater acceptance within the household and community, women went to higher level of social esteem and confidence with the ability to access-own-control assets and decision-making. High level of women-centred economic power resulted in acceptance in the household and this resulted in equity/ equality. Women had more control and say in domestic affairs although this variable varied from community to community.

Blumberg (2005) opines that with economic contributions, there is less domestic violence against women, although in some cases there was an upsurge in domestic violence in the short term as women started becoming self-reliant as this was seen as a threat by the males, but gradually as the economic role of women increased, violence decreased.

On the contrary, Standing (1985) argued that the relationship between economic contribution and increase in women's bargaining power is rarely linear in nature. At times, an increase in women's income may not result in an increase in the total household income. This is because men may withdraw more than their own contribution for their luxury expenditure, with women's income acting as a substitute. Such situations could encourage men to take less responsibility towards household welfare than before. This increases women's vulnerability and has an unsustainable impact on household wellbeing.

Ranade and Ramachandra (1970), and Bannerjee (1999) found, on the basis of the causes of work participation of women in unorganized sector, that poverty is the main compulsion behind their employment.

Studies from both developing and developed countries consistently show about mother's control over resources and impact on child wellbeing. When mothers' control over resources increases, households allocate more resources to children's health and education.[20]

Increase in women's unearned income (pensions, social security, workers' compensation, rent, assets, and gifts) relative to that of men increase per capita caloric intake and children's nutritional status (weight-for-height z-scores). It also finds large impacts on the probability of child survival.

Thus, in the above controversy, are they applicable to the women for whom work has been a part and parcel of their life. To find out the answer to the question, an empirical investigation of Manipur has been conducted.

The necessary reasons for examining the case of Manipur are:

1. To examine the implications of the international results on the situation of Manipur.
2. To study if there are any peculiarities of Manipur which would have implications for the international scenario.

Objectives

In this background, the present study endeavours:

1. to examine the economic contribution of the women vendors in their respective households;
2. to find out the relative human capital content of them;
3. to evaluate their relative position in the decision-making process of their respective households;
4. to assess the relative intra-household resource allocation; and
5. to assess their relative involvement in the socio-politico-economic process of the State.

Reasons for the Selection of the Study Area

Khwairamband Keithel[21] (SanaKeithel) has been selected for our study due to several reasons.

First, this market has unique characteristics regarding the engagement of women in the socio-economic life of the State.

Secondly, this is the only biggest market in Southeast Asia run by women.

Thirdly, this market place provides a laboratory on what it means to women as a livelihood opportunity.

Fourthly, this market place is the only institution that has been the cornerstone of women's strength, their power to support and nurture themselves and their communities, for millennia.

Lastly, this market may be considered as the only living institution sustained till now right from pre-colonial period and the players in the market are still preserving and maintaining the peculiar elements and ideologies which identify their own culture and traditions.

Here it would be of huge significance to examine the emergence of this market place as an institution[22] and as a geographical factor for *bifurcation.*[23]

The absence of ruggedness and *ipso facto* the location near the then seat of power establishes the emergence of pull factors making this location an agglomerating space. This agglomeration continues till today as exemplified by the various photographs.

When we look at the pictures starting from the early 19th Century with no physical structure but only a network of women gathering in a common place, emerging to one with some portions covered with corrugated sheets in the early 20th Century, then to the full-fledged one of the later part of the 20th Century and finally to a fully modernised one seen today. This speaks of the institutional power of this market place to maintain the network of women over centuries.

Methodology and Sampling

A case study was conducted on the registered women vendors at Sana-Keithel (Khwairamband Keithel), which is the main market centre of Manipur run by women only. The highlight of the Keithel is that its vendor - stalls run by women only. The number of commodities sold by the women vendors, run into thousands, which included handloom products, vegetables, fishes and fruits, etc.[24] At present it has 3171 registered women vendors vending in different trades. The Khwairamband Keithel which is the most important and popular bazaar has 3 main markets. They are:

1. Ima Keithel,
2. Laxmi Keithel, and
3. New Market/Linthoingambi Keithel.

Purana Bazar/Ima Keithel

At present, Purana Bazar is popularly known as Ima Keithel (Ima-Mother). It is the largest part of Khwairamband Keithel. Maharaja Chandrakirti Singh (1834-1844; 1850-1886) established this bazaar on 30th May 1869 after levelling the embankment of Thangmeiband.[25] It takes one month to develop the actual framework of Khwairamband Keithel. After completion, on June 1, 1869, the Maiba (Priest) and Maibis (Priestess) carried out the inaugural function of the market.[26]

In the beginning, marketing were generally conducted in the open air. In 1892, the Britishers erected some huts, roofed with thatched meant for market women.[27] As there were frequent occurrences of fire[28] in this market place, it was the then Political Agent Kernel J. Shakespeare (1905-1908; 1909-1914) later roofed with corrugated iron sheets on 6th October 1905.[29]

Laxmi Keithel

Laxmi Keithel is situated on the south-eastern direction of the Ima Keithel. This market is almost an extension of Linthoingambi Keithel. Although the British Government established the Ima Keithel, yet sufficient arrangement was to be made in order to meet the increasing population of Manipur. Moreover, there was a great demand on the part of the women sellers to sit in the market areas of Khwairamband. Thus there was an unduly growth of number of women sitting in and around the ground on which the present Laxmi Keithel was developed.[30]

Formerly, in this market place women were vending fish, fermented fish, utensils and other edible items. Later on, to meet the unduly demand of the women vendors the new construction of the Laxmi Keithel was started in April 1954 and had been completed in April 1956 within two years.[31] At present, the women vendors in this market shed deals mainly with clothes, utensils for ritual purposes and local lamp.

New Market/Linthoingambi Keithel

It is located on the eastern side of the Ima Keithel. The women vending in this market place deals mainly with cloths. Due to the increasing number of cloth sellers, it became overcrowded in the market areas of Khwairamband.[32] Hence, in order to develop a new market, preparations were made to shift the old Johnstone School, which was lying, on the west of the Imphal Civil Hospital to the present Johnstone Higher Secondary compound.[33] This arrangement is also reflected in the resolution of the Imphal Town Fund Committee[34] dated on 19/9/1948. In accordance with the Resolution No. dated 19/6/1948 of the Imphal Town Fund Committee, the old Johnstone was shifted to the present Johnstone Higher Secondary compound. And the new bazaar was constructed on the site of the former Johnstone School.

On the completion of the new Bazar the women vendors who

were mainly Phiyonbis (cloth sellers) belonging to the seven potphams, namely Mayanglang Phijoi Yonpham, Ngabong Yonpham, Phigol Yonpham, Gamsha Yonpham, Rui Yonpham, Pungou Phanek Yonpham and Muga Yonpham of the old Laxmi Keithel were instructed to sit to the newly constructed market known by the named "The New Market".[35] On 25th May, 1990 the members of the Imphal Municipal Board gave the name "Linthoingambi Keithel", who initially proposed many names like Linthoingambi Bazar, Linthoingambi Sana Keithel, Nupi Keithel, Tongou Keithel, Leimarel Keithel etc. After discussion and deliberation, the members of the Imphal Municipal Board, finally resolved to call "The New Market" as "Linthoingambi Keithel".[36] The Municipality took up the resolution for the construction of new sheds of the Linthoingambi Keithel during the period of 1990-1992. It was under section 1960 of the Manipur Municipal Act 1967, that the Government of Manipur approved the construction of new sheds.[37]

Its present detail structure is shown in the following table:

Sl No.	*Name of the market*	*Number of sheds*	*Total no of women vendors*
1	Ima Market	28	1088
2	Laxmi Bazar	14	830
3	New Market/Linthoingambi Keithel	14	1253
	Total	56	3171

Source: Registrar Book, Imphal Municipal Council.
Purana Bazaar: Registrar Book No.1-28.
New Market: Registrar Book No. 1-14.
Laxmi Bazaar: Registrar Book No. 1-14.

We did a random sampling of the three markets to select a 10 per cent sample for detailed survey. We then selected 100 vendors from Ima Market, 80 vendors from Laxmi Bazar and 120 vendors from Linthoingambi Keithel. These work out to be 9.6 per cent from Ima Market, 9.5 per cent from Panthoibi Keithel and 9.5 per cent from Linthoingambi Keithel of the total numbers of vendors in the respective market.

The sample size comprised of 300 women registered vendors of Khwairamband Keithel (Sana-Keithel) of different trades from three different markets. The foundation of the analysis of the present study, however, shall be survey which will be conducted specifically for the purpose. The principal survey instrument was a structured questionnaire administered in August 2007 to women vendors in Khwairamband Keithel over two months. The questionnaire contained a mix of open-ended and limited choice questions covering respondents demographic and socioeconomic background; their reasons for joining the work force, travel arrangement to the market, child care and general levels of satisfaction with their working and living conditions. The questionnaire was supplemented by personal interview without structured questionnaire to allow ample room for the free and frank discussion.

Conclusion

We are in an epoch when women studies are gaining increasing importance both theoretically and empirically. In the beginning, there were more of air and heat, and less of light. But in the last two to three decades, there has undergone a tremendous change in the subject. Besides scholars with different disciplinary backgrounds, the subject is now the focus of all the significant international bodies. As a result of this, the subject is now marked more by light and substance with the areas needing further research more clearly defined.

One finding which has emerged powerfully from these studies is the prevalence of women's face in poverty. In this context the necessity is being emphasized of enhancing the social, economic and political position of women through multiple approaches for equalization of opportunities. Given the global scenario of research, there is need for appreciating the picture of Manipur with the objective of identifying the similarities and the differences.

NOTES & REFERENCES

1. UN (1995): 4th World Conference on Women, Beijing.
2. Social exclusion in general and exclusion of women are now rapidly

emerging areas of research. See, for instance, Devicienti, F. and Poggi, A., (2007), *Poverty and Social Exclusion: Two Sides of the Same Coin or Dynamically Interrelated Processes?*, Laboratorio Riccardo Revelli, (LABOR), Working Paper No. 62; Rodríguez, F. (2008), *What Makes Growth Shared? On the Political Economy of Inclusive Development,* Paper presented at the Annual Bank Conference on Development Economics, South Africa; World Economic Forum, (2009), *Global Gender Gap Report 2009*, Geneva.

3. Gender inequalities exist in almost all societies. Relative to men, women tend to have less access to resources, rights and voice. This disadvantage for women may exist even in cases where male outcomes are relatively poorer (e.g., school enrolment rates in much of Latin America and the Caribbean). Women's empowerment is closely linked with gender equality, because having the agency to choose among options is critically tied to having the options in the first place (World Development Report, 2006). For more detailed about empowerment and its development outcomes one may refer Dollar and Kraay (2002), Kaufmann, Kraay, and Mastruzzi (2004), Moore and Putzel (1999), Bourguignon, Ferreira, and Menendez (2003), Alsop and Norton (2004), Eyben (2003), Moser and Norton (2001),Alsop, Bertelsen, and Holland (2006), Lokshin and Ravallion (2005), Varshney (2005), Stern, Dethier, and Rogers (2005), Sen (1997), Asthana (1996), Couto (1998), Karl(1995), Weissberg (2000).

4. Chen, N., Conconi, P., Peironi, P., (2007): *Women's Earning Power and Double Burden of Market and Household Work*, SOEP papers, German Institute for Economic Research, Berlin, p.1. For more detailed see Altonji and Blank (1999) for a survey on employment and gender gaps for the US, and Blau and Kahn (2003) and Olivetti and Petrongolo (2006) for international comparisons of wage gender gaps.

5. Heineck, G. (2004). "Does religion influence the labour supply of married women in Germany?" *Journal of Socio-Economics*, Vol.33, No. 3, pp. 307-328. Religion is among the most significant factors influencing female labour force participation across countries. See Tzannatos (1999), "Women and Labor Market Changes in the Global Economy: Growth Helps, Inequalities Hurt and Public Policy Matters." *World Development*, Vol. 27, No. 3, pp. 551-569; Dollar and Gatti, (1999), "Gender Inequality, Income and Growth: Are Good Times Good for Women?" *World Bank Policy Research Report* on Gender and Development, Working Paper No.1, World Bank, Washington, D.C.

6. Morrison, Andrew, and Lamana, F., (2006), *Gender Issues in the Kyrgyz Labour Market*, Background paper for Kyrgyz Poverty Assessment, *World Bank*, Washington, D.C. For an economic analysis of gender inequality in the labour market, see Elson, D., (1999), "Labor Markets as Gendered Institutions: Equality, Efficiency and Empowerment Issues." *World Development*, Vol. 27, No. 3, pp. 611.For examples of these inequalities, see Chapter 3, "Religion and Women's Human Rights", in Whitman, P., (1997), ed. , *Religion and Contemporary Liberalism*, University of Notre Dame Press, Notre Dame, pp. 93-137, also in Nussbaum, M., (1999), *Sex and Social Justice*, Oxford University Press, New York.
7. Sen, A., (1999), *Development as Freedom*, Oxford University Press, New York.
8. See Morrison, A., Raju, D., Sinha, D., (2007), Gender Equality, Poverty and Economic Growth, Poverty Reduction and Economic Management Network, *Working Paper No. 4349*. For various explanations for an economic history of female labour force participation see, among others, Goldin (1990), Galor and Weil (1996), Costa (2000), Jones, Manuelli, and McGrattan (2003), Greenwood, Seshadri, and Yorukoglu (2005), Gayle and Golan (2006), Albanesi and Olivetti (2006, 2007).
9. Malhotra, M., (2004), *Empowerment of Women*, Vol. 3, p. 167.
10. Gupta, M., (2004), "Indicators of Women's Development," in Gupta, M., (2004), ed., *Economic Participation of Women*, Vol.1, Sarup and Sons, New Delhi, p. 72
11. *Selected Works of Jawaharlal Nehru*, Orient Longmans.
12. About empowerment, growth, and poverty reduction see especially WDR (2000/2001), Stern, N., (2001), *A Strategy for Development*, World Bank; Ravallion (2001), *Growth, Inequality and Poverty: Looking Beyond Average*, Development Research Group, World Bank, Washington, D.C; Appleton, Simon, Emwanu,T., Kagugube, J., and Muwonge. J., (1999), *Changes in Poverty in Uganda, 1992–1997*, Centre for the Study of African Economies, Oxford, U.K; and Wodon, Q., (1997), "Food Energy Intake and Cost of Basic Needs: Measuring Poverty in Bangladesh" *Journal of Development Studies*, Vol.34, pp. 66–101.
13. Shah, S. (2006), "Sexual Division of Labour in Adam Smith's Work", *Journal of the History of Economic Thought*, Vol.28, pp. 221-241.
14. Goldin, C., (2006), "The Quiet Revolution that Transformed

Women's Employment, Education and Family", *American Economic Review*, Vol.96, pp. 1-21.

15. See Schuler, S.R. and Hashemi, S.M., (1994), "Credit Programs, Women's Empowerment, and Contraceptive Use in Rural Bangladesh," *Studies in Family Planning*, Vol. 25, No. 2, pp. 65-76; Hashemi, S.M., Schuler, S. R., and Riley, A. P., (1996), "Rural Credit Programs and Women's Empowerment in Bangladesh," *World Development*, Vol. 24, pp. 635-653; Zaman, H., (1999), *Assessing the Poverty and Vulnerability Impact of Micro-Credit in Bangladesh: A Case Study of BRAC*, World Bank, Washington, D.C.; and Kabeer, N., (2001), "Conflicts over Credit: Re-Evaluating the Empowerment Potential of Loans to Women in Rural Bangladesh," *World Development*, Vol. 29, pp. 63-84.

16. For an interesting survey in this area, see, Murduck (1949), Boserup (1970), Matthiassen (1974), Bossen (1975), Devi Lalitha (1982), Sharma (1983), Bardhan (1985), Sesodia (1985), Singh and Singh (1987), Singh (1988), Yale Sulvia (1989), Deniz (1990), Jemol (1990), Dianiel (1990), Diwan (1995), Jones (1999).

17. See Blood and Wolfe (1960), Morgan (1975), Majumder (1978), Saikia (1980), Scanjoni (1980), Patel (1984), Jain (1985), Malladi (1985), Desai (1987), Murdock and Leistritz (1988).

18. See Klein, V., (1965), Britain Married Women Workers, Routledge and Kegan Paul, London; and Schmid, G. (1984), *Sex Discrimination and Equal Opportunity: The Labor Market and Employment Policy*, Palgrave Macmillan.

19. See Blackden, C. M., and Wodon, (2006), Gender, Time Use and Poverty in Sub-Saharan Africa, *Working Paper No. 73*, World Bank, Washington, DC.

20. Please refer, Rubalcava et al. (2004), Pitt et al.(2003), Duflo (2003), Quisumbing and Maluccio (2003), Hoddinott and Haddad (1995), Schultz, P., (1990), Thomas, D., (1990).

21. The concept of market runs parallel to that of Manipuri word "Keithel". The term "Keithel" is the combination of two Manipuri words "Kei" or store and "Thel" or display meaning display of store-house for the exchange of goods either through barter system or money circulation.

22. We are using this term from the angle of New Institutional Economics. For an exposition on this see North, D., (1990), *Institutions, Institutional Change and Economic Performance: Political economy of Institutions and Decisions*, Cambridge

University Press; and North, D., Wallis, J., and Weingast, B., (2006), *A Conceptual Framework for Interpreting Recorded Human History,* Working Paper No. 12795, National Bureau of Economic Research, December, http://www.nber.org/papers/w12795. For an exposition of this with an attempt to apply to the issues of North East India, see Yumnam, A., (2009), *North East: Time To Move from Nash Equilibrium to Specialist Equilibrium,* Presidential Address delivered at the 11th Annual Conference of the North Eastern Economic Association held at the Indian Institute of Technology, Guwahati, December.

23. We mean by this the emergence of a location as an agglomerating space in the sense used by New Economic Geographers. In this connection, see Krugman, P., (1991), "Increasing Returns and Economic Geography", *Journal of Political Economy,* Vol. 99, pp. 483-499; and Fujita, M., Krugman, P., and Venables, A., (1999), *The Spatial Economy: Cities, Regions and International Trade,* Cambridge University Press. In this approach, an initial economic shock can launch any geographical space to bifurcate from other adjoining areas.

24. Ahluwalia, B.K., (1984), "The Land of Jewels", in Ahluwalia, B.K., and Shashi Ahluwalia, ed., *Social Change in Manipur,* (1984), Cultural Publishing House, New Delhi , p. 17.

25. Ibungohal and Khelchandra (1967), *Cheitharol Kumbaba,* ed., Imphal, p. 18.

26. Dun, E.W. (1975), *Gazetteer of Manipur,* Vivek Publishing House, Delhi, p. 64.

27. Singh, L.J. (1995), The Lost Kingdom, First Edition, p.242.

28. The frequent occurrence of fire was mainly due to the reason that the women sellers used kerosene lamps or pinewood for lighting at night. See Ibungohal and Khelchandra (1967).

29. Ibungohal and Khelchandra (1967), *op. cit.,* p. 551.

30. Indramani, N., (2007), Puwarida Eikhoigi Keithelgi Machat, Ma ong – Ma touAmadi Chiraba Tanphamda Keithel Nupisingna Loukhiba Thoudang, A seminar paper presented on 26th October 2008, Kangla Hall, Imphal.

31. *Evolutionary Growth of the Khwairamband Keithel,* Compiled by Manipur Research Society, 7th September 2003, p.17.

32. *Ibid.,* p.16.

33. *The Bheigapati Patrika,* a daily paper, 19th March 1948.

34. It was a committee to look after the affairs of the British reserve areas, since 1915. See *Administrative Report of 1915-16.*

    In 1956, the Government of Manipur introduced Assam Municipality Act, 1923 and the Town Fund Committee was converted into Imphal Municipality in 1956 covering a Municipal area of 1.20 sq. miles. Please refer *Evolutionary Growth of the Khwairamband Keithel* (2003).

35 Arrangement was made in accordance with Imphal Town Fund Committee's Resolution No.3, dated 30/12/53. In its Resolution No.2 dated 5/1/54 and Notification dated 6/1/54 the Town Fund ordered phiyonbis of the above potphams to shift to the "New Market".

36. *Imphal Municipal Board,* Resolution No. 1 of the proceeding of the Imphal Municipal Board, dated 25/5/90.

37. Government of Manipur, Letter No. 6/99/4 RBI/DEV/85 (Vol.-IV), 2nd September 1990 and Office of the Imphal Municipal Board-Resolution No. 5(2), dated 14th September 90.

2

Women in Manipur

Introduction

Manipur, a tiny and hilly State, formerly a feudal kingdom, with an area of 22,327 sq. km. is located at the crossroads of South, Southeast and Far East Asia comprising of a central valley and its surrounding hills and have been a melting pot of waves of people and their cultures.

Like the other North-Eastern States of India, its topography too is undulating and characterized by numerous hillocks, plains, valleys, rivers, etc. other than forest cover. The Manipur valley is a cradle of human civilisation, and Alfred Lyall describes it as "an oasis of comparative civilisation amidst the barbarians."[1] It is famous in the world for its natural beauty, cultural heritage and costumes, dances, arts and crafts, courageous and hard working women.

To understand the spirit of a civilization and to appreciate its excellences and realize its limitations is to study the history of the position and status of women. Therefore, to facilitate appreciation of the present status and position of the women of Manipur, we shall give a general picture on the relative status and position during the pre (before 1891) and the post-colonial (1891-1947) rule.

Looking Back at the Historical Trend

In order to better appreciate the status and position of Manipuri women during the pre-and post-colonial period, it is incumbent on our part to examine here the economic role they played during the period. The Manipuri women remained, because of their economic role and the status they enjoyed in the society, a subject of admiration for the foreigners, sociologists and anthropologists who visited Manipur. Captain E.W. Dun in his book, '*The Gazetteer of Manipur*' commented thus: "They [Women of Manipur] are very industrious. The most of the work of the country except the heaviest is performed by them. It would be difficult to find a more industrious woman in India than the Manipuri".[2] Mrs Grimwood also spoke of the condition and virtues of Manipuri women in her book '*My Three Years in Manipur*', "The Manipuri do not shut up their women, as is the custom in most parts of India, and they are much more enlightened and intelligent in consequence".[3] James Johnstone also shares views about the Manipuri women's economic role in his book '*Manipur and Naga Hills*', "Women are the great traders and many would walk miles in the morning and buy things in the more distant bazaars to sell again in the capital in the evening."[4] The ideal woman in this country (Manipur) was described as hard working in the rice field, efficient with children, devoted to religion and a shrewd business woman in the market.[5]

Women's Position during Pre-Colonial Period

Ester Boserup[6] contends that in the pre-industrial economies, growth of population promotes technological change by making it possible to raise capital formation and volume of investments in expanding production. In such an economy, population growth is taken as an autonomous change. In the light of these considerations, the steady increase in population in Manipur from 1872-1881 might be seen as an indication of the steady progress in productive activities. Table 2.1 provides a picture of the population growth of Manipur during the pre-colonial period for which census figures are available.

Growth of Population

According to the Census of 1872 Manipur had a population of 1,26,000 persons which rose to 2,21,070 persons in 1881. So the average annual rate of increase population between 1872 and 1881 was 7.5 per cent. While some proportion of the rise could be attributed, as elsewhere, to better coverage of the census exercise in 1881, the fact of a substantial growth of population remains as evidenced from the natural growth rates in this and the subsequent censuses. As regards the relative shares of male and female in

1881 census, it is of equi-proportionality with a very marginal higher proportion of female, i.e., 49.56 per cent male and 50.44 per cent female of the total.

Table 2.1: Population of Manipur (1872-1881)

Population / Year	*1872**	*1881*		
		Male	*Female*	*Total*
Population	1,26,000	1,09,557 (49.56 %)	1,11,513 (50.44 %)	2,21,070 (100%)

*Sex distribution of population is not available for this year.

Source: *Census of India*, 1881

Sex Ratio (Females per 1000 Males)

Table 2.2 presents the sex ratio of Manipur during pre-colonial period. Females which constitute over 50 per cent of the population in 1881, its sex ratio was also in favour of females with 1,018 females per thousand males. Females outnumbering the males during this period could be the polygamous trend of the royalty and nobility.

Table 2.2: Sex Ratio of Manipur (1881Census)

Year	*Total Sex Ratio*
1881	1,018

Development of Education

Creation of educational opportunities was an important development during the tenure of Sir James Johnstone as Political Agent (1877-1886) in Manipur. The first school was, however, started in 1872 'at the suggestion of Major – General W.F. Nuthall', the then Political Agent.[7] The King and his Durbar were not, however, enthusiastic about this move for the obvious apprehension that with the spread of education among people, the pressure for social, political and economic reforms would mount.[8] As a result, the school was nearly closed.

The proposal for starting a school at Imphal was revived by Johnstone during his period as Political Agent of the British Empire in Manipur. He succeeded in obtaining the consent of the King to establish an English school in 1885. In the beginning, of course, only a small number of students attended the school. But their number slowly increased. Development of the modern institutional form of education had come to stay though in the beginning it was male who attended the school.[9]

Provisions were also there to give education to the Manipuri girls right from the early stage of modern education. In one source, the First Girls' School was started as early as 1889-90.[10] In another source, it was found that the female education got its momentum only after the British administration of Manipur. The Primary school for girls was opened on December, 1899 with 12 pupils and this number increased to 53 at the end of the year.[11] By the turn of 20th century, there was a slow but perceptible change in attitude of the local population to the western education and so an increasing number of students - both boys and girls- beginning to attend schools. Quite naturally more and more schools were started.[12]

Although there was a slow progress in education during the early period, women's role in the socio-economic process of the State was of vital importance as discussed below.

Economic Status of Women[13]

A glimpse of the economic status of Manipuri women during the pre- colonial period can be had from the occupational structure of the population, which is given in Table 2.2.

In Table 2.2 we present a picture of male and female proportion in different categories of occupation. As seen from this table it is found that the proportion of both male and female is more or less the same with 49.56 per cent in the case of male and 50.44 per cent in the case of female being engaged in different occupations as per the 1881 Census.

We can also examine this table (Table 2.3) from two angles, one from the angle of within category (male/female) and another from differences between the two sexes. First, the inter-sex differences in occupation come out glaringly in professional class and commercial class; while in the case of other categories the relative shares are more or less the same between the two sexes.

Female's share in agricultural class is more or less the same with males' share which imply no simple gender division of labour with regard to crop production. The relative share of male in industrial class is double its females' share with 69.9 per cent male and 30.1 per cent female of their relative total. Females constitute the highest proportion in commercial class with 96.3 per cent between the sexes and male constituting the highest proportion in professional class with 80.9 per cent between the sexes. Males' proportion is nearly about 4 times its female proportion in the professional class.

Table 2.3: Distribution of Occupational Structure by Sex (1881Census)

Sl.No./ Numbers	*Occupation*[14]	*Total*	*Male*	*Percent*	*Female*	*Percent*
	I	*II*	*III*	*IV*	*V*	*VI*
1	Professional class	15,027	12,169 (11.1%)	80.9	2,858 (2.6%)	19.1
2	Domestic class	14,996	7,324 (6.7%)	48.8	7,672 (6.9%)	51.2
3	Commercial class	15,433	572 (0.5%)	3.7	14,861 (13.4%)	96.3
4	Agricultural class	1,03,937	51,057 (46.6%)	49.1	52,880 (47.4%)	50.9
5	Industrial class	3,042	2,125 (1.9%)	69.9	917 (0.8%)	30.1
6	Indefinite and non-productive class	68,635	36,310 (33.2%)	52.9	32,310 (28.9%)	47.1
	Total	2,21,070	1,09,557 (100)	49.56	1,11,513 (100)	50.44

Note: The figures within parentheses are the percentages of the relevant total male and female column totals, while figures in columns IV and VI are respective shares of male and female in the relevant raw category.

Source: The above table is extracted from the figures given in Dun, E.W., (1886), *Gazetteer of Manipur*, Reprinted by Vivek Publishing Company, (1981) Delhi.

In the other case of within category comparisons, the table (Table 2.3) reveals that Agricultural class constitutes the highest proportion in male with 46.6% of their relevant total. It was followed by Category 6(Indefinite and non-productive class) with 33.2 per cent of their relevant total. Category 1 (Professional class) then followed it with 11.1 per cent, Category 5 (Industrial class) with 1.9 per cent and Category 2 (Domestic class) with 6.7 per cent of their relevant total. The lowest proportion in male is found in Category 3 (Commercial class) with only 0.5 per cent of their relevant total. This low percentage of the commercial category and as compared to the high proportion of women in this very category speaks volumes of the participation of the women in market activities. While the women are generally confined within the four walls of the home in most societies of comparable development levels, Manipur wore an altogether different picture with the women participating and even dominating in the trading sector.

In the case of female, the table also depicts that the shares of female in Agricultural class with 47.4 per cent is the highest of all the occupational classes. It is then followed by Category 3 (Commercial class) constituting a proportion of 13.4 per cent, Category 2 (Domestic class) with 6.9 per cent and Category 1(Professional class) with 2.6 per cent of their relevant total. The least proportion in female is found in Category 5 (Industrial class) with only 0.8 per cent of their relevant total. A joint interpretation of the female and proportions in different activities speaks of the more or less equal participation of both the sexes in economic activities.

Role of Manipuri Women

The Manipuri women have been taking a crucial role in the social, political and economic development through ages. Even though it is a part of the legend, it reflects the trend of the mentality of the society.[15] Here, an emphasis has been made to explore the social status of women in Manipur during historical period. Because, the past, if it can be located, contains the key to the present.

The courage and hard labour of Manipuri Women has been considered to be unique from pre-historical times. They made crucial economic contributions and they were the mainstay of the family circle.[16]

As seen above from Table 2.2 the Manipuri women were extremely industrious, and used to perform the productive activities related to agriculture, animal husbandry, cottage industry and internal trade, besides the domestic chores. These constituted the mainstay of the Meitei (Manipuri) economy. For these reasons the role of women is considered by the analysts to have been of vital importance in keeping the superstructure of Meitei state growing and expanding over time.

In 1886, Dun mentioned in his highly referred book the type of freedom in occupational participation in production and exchange activities enjoyed by the women of Manipur. He observed: "... all the marketing is done by the women, all the works of buying and selling in public, carrying to and fro of articles to be sold, whilst at home, they busy employed in weaving and spinning".[17] A continuation of this age-old tradition is recorded by modern (late-twentieth century observers as well. These scholars highlight the women of Manipur conducting "their business with perfect confidence and competence. They present the picture of women who know that they too are bread winners, which they don't have to fight, like their counterparts in the so-called developed nations, for liberation".[18]

Having realised that women have been playing an active role in the conduct of various economic activities in the land, we may now look at the scenario of the various activities separately. Agriculture is a family enterprise in Meitei villages. Rice was, as it is today, the main agricultural crop of Manipur during the pre-colonial days. It was grown mainly by using the method of transplantation of seedlings. Women worked longer hours than men did in the paddy field. They would start their engagement in the field from early morning and for a better part of the day. They would involve themselves in preparing fields, sowing seeds, nurturing seedbeds, transplanting seedlings, and weeding, etc. For harvesting crops, which called for mobilization of a large work force, men joined women for early completion of the work. Vegetable gardening for domestic consumption as well as for exchange was also a major activity for women. This scenario of women working longer hours than men in the fields is labelled "female farming system" by Ester Boserup.[19]

Besides working in the field, women of Manipur were also active in animal husbandry and in spinning and weaving clothes. Selling surplus agricultural, horticultural and household industrial products and buying goods for family's consumption and meeting other needs felt within the exclusive domain of women.[20] All these indicate, to reemphasise, that the role of women in Manipur society had been salient right from early stages.

It has been found from a study of global scenario that, in times of distress when the family starts suffering declines in social rankings, it is generally the women who would shed all taboos and barriers of work. They would take on any earning opportunity, which the men folk would generally shy away, they come across to support the family.[21]

This behavioural perspective gets reflected in the functioning's of women folks of Manipur as well from the early stages onwards.

Manipur had, during the periods of Kingdom, an institution known as "Lallup-Kaba"[22] under which the men-folk were not available for a few days for family work or otherwise as they had to devote themselves exclusively to the service of the state (king). During the period of absence of the men-folk, the family had however to be maintained, and this onus naturally felt on the women-folk. There is a widely held opinion that this institution of service to the king was push factor for the women to take part in familial economic activities.[23] While we may not go to the extent of attributing the economic participation of women to the prevalence of this institution, we can safely say that it must have reinforced the already prominent presence of women in the performance of various economic activities in the society. This alternative perspective arises from the fact that during the period of Lallup the family did not have to pay the revenue to the state. It would have been possible for the family to live on this saved revenue during the period of absence of the men-folk, but it did not. On the contrary, the women did come out and take on economic activities on their own. It speaks volumes of the inherent orientation of the women-folk towards work ıather than idling around as routine housewives.

Since the early days, women of Manipur have been playing an active role in the political affairs of the state and they took part in administration as well. The heritage of women's participation in the war continued up to the 18th century. The princesses and queens occasionally led the royal army and undertook conquests of neighbouring hill tribes and thereby earned fame.[24]

Position of Manipuri during Colonial Rule, 1891-1947

After the fierce Anglo-Manipuri War of 1891, the de facto powers of administration of Manipur fell in the hands of British officers.[25] Direct British intervention in the administration of Manipur laid the foundation for significant changes in the socio-cultural values and attitudes of the people and consequently in their economic pursuits as well; these were to have lasting implications for the socio-politico-economic structure and are being felt till today. The concomitant economic changes were marked by the growth of population, development of human resources through spread of literacy and education among the Manipuri youths, new kind of farm practices and processing of farm and forests products and growing volume of monetary transactions in lieu of the traditional exchanges of commodities for commodities and labour services. Naturally the roots for diversification in occupational pattern were laid during this period. We must, however, add here that such changes, though salient, were taking place at a rather slow pace, maybe because of the contemporary socio-economic milieu. In what follows in this and the following chapters, we would be examining as to whether these changes reinforced or alter the traditional participation of Manipuri women in various occupations. For this purpose we shall depend on the relevant census Reports which contain valuable statistics about the demographic development and the occupational structure of the population.

Growth of Population

We have already noted that the importance of population growth in promoting capital accumulation which in turn improves production. Here an account of population growth in Manipur during the colonial period is provided.

In Table 2.4, we present a picture of the trend of Manipur's population growth from 1901-1941, i.e., during the colonial period by sex. As seen from the table, the relative size of male and female had remained more or less the same over the years. As regards the rate of population growth, during 1901-1911 it registered a decadal growth rate of 21.71 per cent but it declined to 10.92 per cent in the decade of 1911-1921. The growth rate, however, recovered to 16.04 per cent during 1921-1931 and 14.92 per cent during 1931-1941. As per the Census Report of 1931, the fall in the growth rate in the decade 1911-1921 was confined to the hill areas - which suffered terrible 'havoc wrought by the influenza epidemic'. Another factor responsible was the Kuki rebellion of 1917-19 that unsettled the tribal population in the affected area.[26]

Figure 2.1 illustrate the sex wise growth of population of Manipur from 1901 to 1941.

Sex Ratio (Females per thousand Males)

Sex ratio is considered to be one of the most important indicators of the status of women in any society. In this section we endeavour to provide a picture of the sex ratio of Manipur from 1901-1941.

Table 2.4: Growth of Population of Manipur, 1901-1941

(Area: 8628 sq. miles)

Year	*Male*	*Female*	*Decadal rate of growth of population (per cent)*
1901	49.1	50.9	-
1911	49.3	50.7	21.71
1921	48.9	51.1	10.92
1931	48.4	51.6	16.04
1941	48.7	51.3	14.92

Source: Census Reports, 2001

The Table 2.4 reveals that throughout the colonial period (1901-1941) the sex ratio remained in favour of the female with the ratio rising further towards the end of the period. The sex ratio started off with 1,037 in 1901 and the colonial period terminated with the figure of 1,055. The highest sex-ratio recorded

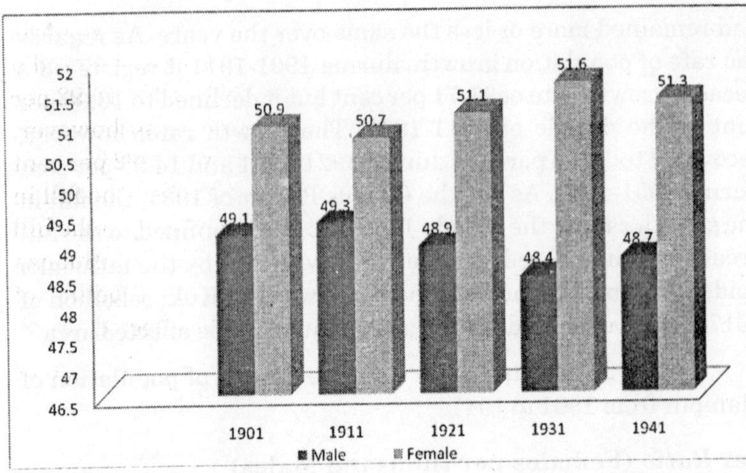

Figure 2.1: Sex-wise Growth of Population of Manipur, 1901-1941

was 1,065 of 1931 Census. In the case of urban the highest sex ratio could be found in the year 1931 with 1,137 which was also higher than the overall sex ratio of the State. In the case of rural the highest is found in the same year 1931 with the sex ratio of 1,048.

One interesting feature emanating from Table 2.5 is the relative position of sex ratios of the rural and the urban areas. The period started with more or less similar sex ratios in 1901 but the urban ratio kept on surpassing the rural ratio for all the colonial years. In other words, the ratios of rural sex ratio to urban sex ratio were 1.02 in 1911, 1.06 in 1921, and 1.08 in 1931 though it reduced slightly to 1.05 in 1941. This trend is a situation which is quite contrary to the global scenario. The normal situation globally encountered during development trajectory is one where the urban sex ratio turns out to be definitely unfavourable to women, mainly due to emigration of male from rural to urban areas. The scenario in Manipur was just opposite to this. An enquiry into this would constitute a rewarding area for social science research but is beyond the scope of this book.

Figure 2.2 shows the complete picture of sex ratio of Manipur during the colonial period, 1901-1941.

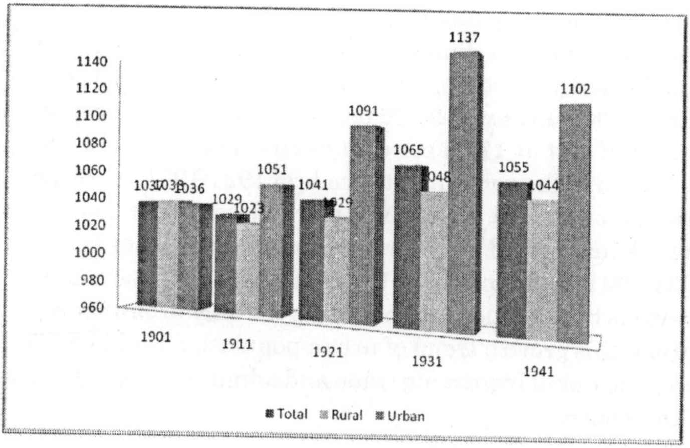

Figure 2.2: Sex Ratio of Manipur by Rural and Urban, 1901-1941

Growth Rates of Rural and Urban Population of Manipur, 1901-1941

Table 2.5 presents a picture of the growth rates of rural and urban population of Manipur for the period from 1901 to 1941.

Table 2.5: Growth Rate of Rural and Urban Population (1901-1941)

Year	*Total*	*Rural*	*Urban*
1901	1,037	1,038	1,036
1911	1,029	1,023	1,051
1921	1,041	1,029	1,091
1931	1,065	1,048	1,137
1941	1,055	1,044	1,102

Source: *Census of India, 2001*

As seen from the Table 2.6 the growth rate of rural population of Manipur declined in 1911-1921 and 1931-1941 decades, while the urban population of Manipur maintained an increasing trend throughout. We might recall here the picture which emerged from the analysis of overall population growth during the same period. It was seen in Table 2.3 that the State suffered a decline in population growth rate during 1911-1921 due to the influenza epidemic and the Kuki rebellion. The fact that the brunt of the decline was borne by the rural areas is amply established by Table 2.5. While the growth rate of rural population during 1901-1911 was 27.96 per cent, it declined sharply to less than half of it at 11.95 per cent during 1911-1921. It, however, recovered in the subsequent decade of 1921-1931. As regards the urban growth rate, it showed a marked rise in the last decade of the colonial period by recording a rate of 16.12 per cent during 1931-1941 as compared to the rate of around 7 per cent in the previous two decades. Imphal being the only urban centre of the period, this growth trend of urban population could be taken as the indicator of increasing trade and administrative importance of this centre.

Table 2.6: Percentage Variation of Population of Manipur, 1901-1941

	1901-1911	*1911-1921*	*1921-1931*	*1931-1941*
Total	+21.71	+10.92	+16.04	+14.92
Rural	+27.96	+11.95	+18.35	+14.61
Urban	+3.34	+7.17	+7.25	+16.21

Source: The Office of the Registrar General and Census Commissioner of India as given in *Basic Statistics of North Eastern Region, 2006*, North Eastern Council, p.3.

Literacy Rate

Table 2.7 presents the male-female break-up of literacy rates from 1901[27]-1931.

Table 2.7: Literacy Rate of Manipur from 1901-1931 by Different Age Groups (in per cent)

Year	*10 years and above*		*15-20 years*		*20 years and above*	
	Male	*Female*	*Male*	*Female*	*Male*	*Female*
1901	2.7	0.1	2.2	0.1	3.1	0.1
1911	5.8	0.2	6.6	0.2	6.0	0.2
1921	8.5	0.2	8.2	0.3	9.4	0.2
1931	9.0	0.4	10.5	0.6	9.7	0.3

Source: Mullan, C.S., (1932), *Census of India, 1931, Assam, Part-I,* Report, p.164

Note: Though no specific criterion was provided, the population was divided into two classes of literate and illiterate in the 1901 Census. In the subsequent censuses of 1911, 1921 and 1931, literacy was defined as the ability to write a letter and read the response.

The following main points emerge from Table 2.7:

A. One stark picture emerging from the table is the sharp gender differential in literacy rates.[28] Whereas male literacy rates for all the age groups showed rise in every census, the literacy rates for females across age groups displayed constancy throughout except a negligible rise towards the end of the period. A picture of the rising gender differential (the gap between male and female literacy rates across age groups) is given in Table 2.7A. It is evident from this table that the sex differential in literacy got quadrupled or at least tripled during the period. It speaks volumes of the initial orientation in education provision, appreciation and acceptance in the society.

B. The table also indicates a very low female literacy rate in all the age groups in every census. This could be due primarily to (i) the unimportance attached to female education then; and (ii) the reluctance of the females themselves to attend schools for western education, which was then considered to be impure.[29] Another possible reason could be the subsistence oriented kind of activities among the families which made the simultaneous sacrifice of work by both male and female of a family for attending schools economically unfeasible. Still another possible reason could be the nature of the undiversified labour market then, which was yet to display any characteristic demand for educated women.

Table 2.7A: Gender Differential (Gap between Male and Female) in Literacy Rates, 1901-1931

(in percentage points)

Year	*10 years and above*	*15-20 years*	*20 years and above*
1901	2.6	2.1	3.0
1911	5.6	6.4	5.8
1921	8.3	7.9	9.2
1931	8.6	9.9	9.4

Source: Computed from Table 2.7

Table 2.7B: Sex-wise Literacy Rate of Manipur, 1901-1941

Year of Census	*Percentage of Literacy*		
	Male	*Female*	*Total*
1901	1.86	0.04	0.3
1911	4.04	0.12	2.89
1921	7.65	0.15	3.82
1931	6.40	0.30	3.25
1941	9.77	0.61	5.06

Source: Economic Survey Manipur, 2002-2003, Directorate of Economic and Statistics, Government of Manipur, p.13.

C. The 1941 Census Reports have turned out to be the most difficult ones to come by. Whereas detailed age-group wise information on literacy rates are not available for this Census, unlike the earlier ones, the total literacy rates are, however, available from subsequent censuses. A picture of sex-wise literacy rates from 1901 to 1941 is provided in Table 2.7B. This table can be read together with 2.7B (i) which provides the gender differential of the overall literacy rates calculated on the basis of data given in Table 2.7B. These two tables too speak of the low literacy rate of female. Despite the efforts of forty years, the female literacy rate did not touch even 1 per cent. Still further the gender differential, which was unfavourable to female to

Table 2.7B (i): Gender Differential (Gap between Male and Female) in Literacy Rates, 1901-1941

(in percentage points)

Year of Census	*Gender Differential*
1901	1.82
1911	3.92
1921	7.50
1931	6.1
1941	9.16

*Source: Computed from Table 2.6*B

begin with, kept on worsening over the entire period; the differential in 1941 became almost five times of the 1901 differential.

The sex wise literacy rate of Manipur and the Gender Differential during the colonial period, 1901-1941 are illustrated in figure 2.3 and 2.4 respectively.

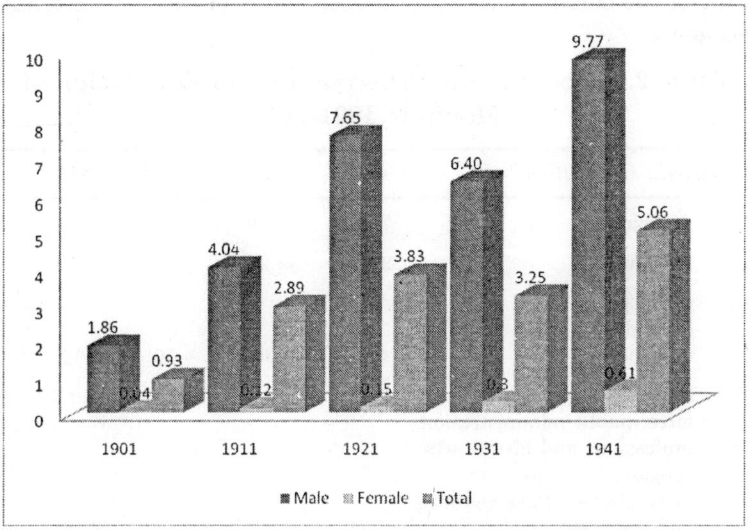

Figure 2.3: Sex-wise Literacy Rate of Manipur, 1901-1941

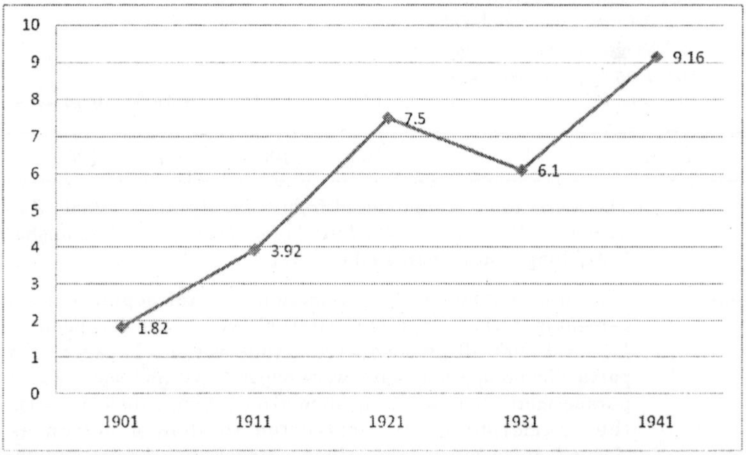

Figure 2.4: Gender Differential (Gap between Male and Female) in Literacy Rates of Manipur, 1901-1941

Occupational Distribution

In this section, we discuss the occupational distribution of population during the colonial period with a view to appreciate the relative occupational engagement of the population. This would not only provide an idea of the economic structure of the period but would as well throw light on the evolving economic structure during the colonial period as a foreshadow of the post-colonial economy.

Table 2.8: Occupational Distribution of Population of Manipur, 1901-1931

Categories	*Occupation*[33]	*1901*	*1911*	*1921*	*1931*
I	Agriculture	72.80	77.70	83.93	79.30
II	Industry	22.10	14.20	8.80	13.68
III	Commerce (including transport)	0.34	4.30	4.50	4.12
IV	Professions(public force, public administration, professions and liberal arts religion, law, medicine, instructions letters and arts and sciences)	1.71	2.00	2.16	2.16
V	Miscellaneous (proprietors other than of agricultural land) funds and scholarship holders, domestic service inmates of jails, asylums, beggars etc.	3.05	1.80	0.61	0.74
	Total	100	100	100	100

Sources: The above table is reproduced from Ganguly, J. B., (2006), *An Economic History of North East India, 1826 to 1947*, Akansha Publishing House, New Delhi, p. 371.

Note: "The above table is the proportion of total population (in percentage terms) supported by (actual workers and dependents). It is not that all persons were actual workers engaged in a particular occupation; some were dependents, and some would pursue more than one occupation. To deal with these realities the enumerators were instructed to show a person as 'dependents' 'whenever the individual in question did not actually work at the occupation shown against his or her name. The rules further laid down that for persons with two or more occupations the chief one only should be entered, except when they are owned or cultivated land in addition to another occupation when both should be recorded'. This pattern was more or less followed for the 1911 and 1921 census also." (Allen, *op.cit.*, p.161)

Table 2.8 gives a summary picture of the proportions of population in different occupations during the period 1901-1931.[30] While interpreting the table we would supplement it with information otherwise not explicitly produced in the table. The following main pictures emerge from the table.

First, it is easily evident that agriculture was the main occupation of the workers by engaging almost more or less 80 per cent of the population throughout the period. Even the lower figure of 1901 has been attributed ".... chiefly due to the fact that no less than 34,304 women have been shown as actual workers under the head of weavers and spinners; little exports of cloth from Manipur, and as total population of that state is only 284,465,it hardly seems probable that over 34,000 Manipuri females can be earning their living by weaving cloths for sale, and the majority of those persons were probably the women folks of agriculturists, who make cloths for home wear, and who in other districts have been included in the cultivating class".[31]

Secondly, commerce continued to maintain its importance in the economy right through the colonial period. In this case the lower proportion in 1901 as compared to the later years of the colonial period, the 1901 census explains it as under-enumeration.[32]

Third, another significance development during the colonial period was the rise in the number of people in professional occupations. Though it looked low and insignificant in terms of proportions of the total population, yet the rise in absolute numbers was discernible by the social standards of the time.

Figure 2.5 shows a diagrammatical representation of the occupational distribution of population of Manipur from 1901 to 1931.

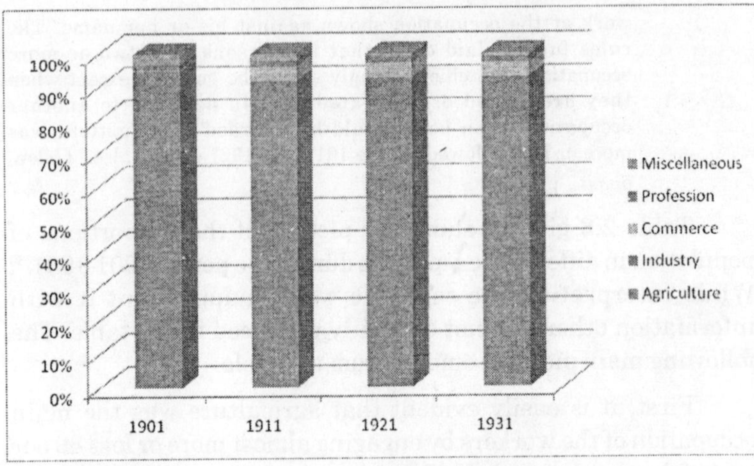

Figure 2.5: Occupational Distribution of Population of Manipur, 1901-1931

Remarkable Events of the Women Folk of Manipur during Colonial Rule

Women of Manipur have an inherent capability to identify strongly with the things they have associated with. This feeling gets manifested in their efforts to sustain whatever they have been living with. We have examples of these in every historical epoch of the land.

This is the reason why they refuse to stay back when any administrative measure poses a threat to their economic welfare. There are ample instances in history when their collective power had altered their administrative course of action.[34]

The first instance relates to the year 1904. On 15th March 1904, a fire in the middle of the night destroyed the bungalow in which Captain Nuttah and Mr. Dunlop lived. Some months later on 4th August of the same year, some unknown persons burnt down the house of Assistant Political Agent. Maxwell, the then Political Agent and Superintendent of the State suspected "political incendiarism".[35]

Maxwell then contemplated giving a warning to the persons responsible for what he thought "political incendiarism". He ordered the rebuilding of the destroyed bungalows with teak wood to be collected from the Kabaw valley (now in Myanmar) with free labour by local male labour. He further declared that, in the event of non-compliance of provision of free labour, a "punitive force" would be stationed in the Imphal and the cost of which will be borne by the local people. This enraged the people who responded with protest meetings and determination to flout the unjust orders. The British authorities suppressed these agitations by arresting some important leaders of the movement who were later exiled from Manipur. Having no alternative, the male members of Imphal yielded to the order and started to rebuild the house.[36]

With the men-folk having failed in their movement for justice, the onus now felt on the women. Here it would be worthwhile to mention the historical context of this failing. This failure of the men's agitation came within one and a half decades of the defeat in the hands of the British. The defeat of 1891 was immediately followed by certain institutional reforms which turned out to be more exploitative than the *Lallup*. The Britishers abolished the Lallup but enforced free labour for construction works, and imposed new taxes besides war compensation. These institutional impositions coupled with the two failures within a span of less than two decades sapped the morale of the men-folk in particular and the society in general. There was thus the need for rekindling the social pride of the Manipuris in which somebody had to play the role. The women-folk did not shirk their responsibility at this socio-historically critical juncture and swung into action. They started collective protests and demonstrations against the order for free labour of the Political Agent. Since the women remained relentless in their protests despite police actions, the British authority had to finally withdraw the orders requiring the Manipuris to rebuild the gutted buildings free of cost.[37] This success, known in history as the *First Nupilal* (First Women's Agitation), could be regarded as a signal boost to the process of empowerment of Manipuri women.

The second instance occurred in 1939 when the administration adopted a policy of allowing export of rice to outside the State by Marwari merchants. This led to rise in the price of the staple food of the people, and taking Manipur almost on the

Picture 2.1: Women demonstrators protesting around the Telegraph Office on 12th December, 1939.[39]

verge of a famine. Women, tradeswomen in particular, organized themselves into a collective, and a massive demonstration was launched against the official policy of exporting rice. Thousands of women from all over the Valley gathered in the capital and completely closed down the Khwairamband Keithel, the main market at Imphal. As the administration failed to respond to their repeated appeals for revoking the rice export order, the women demonstrators ultimately confronted the Durbar in session. They gathered around the office, raised slogans, cried out in strident notes asking the officials to undo the order and reimpose a ban on the export of rice. The members of the Durbar had to flee through the back-door. But Sharpe, the President of the Durbar, was immediately surrounded by the women and had to face them alone. They compelled him to go along to the Telegraph Office and where they confined him along with the Civil Surgeon and other officers of the Telegraph Office. They demanded an order from the Maharaja, who was then away on a pilgrimage, reversing the rice export order. Despite the attempts of the army, led by the Commandant of the 4thAssam Rifles to disperse the protestors, they kept the officers confined to the Telegraph Office till midnight. The administration had but to issue the necessary orders immediately banning the export of rice.[38]This uprising of women is recorded in history as the *Second Nupilal.*

In both the instances cited above, the epicentre of the movement was the women's market in Imphal. Even today, the role of women in these two episodes is narrated with excitement and pride by all Manipuris.

These two landmark movements in the colonial history of Manipur have naturally had tremendous impact on the socio-politico-economic dynamics in the years that followed. These established beyond doubt that women of Manipur do not fight merely for material goals or to increase their participation in the system, but to incorporate cultural meanings in social actions and thereby define the space for politico-administrative action.[40] In other words, women in Manipur do not suffer from the women stand behind men syndrome, but are active observers of the social dynamics around them. The success of these two movements added a new dimension and a new strength to social and political consciousness among the people while at the same establishing that the Britishers were not free from susceptibility. This new social reality led to the emergence of a new class of political workers not bound by the psychological limits of the recent failures. The catalyst of these changes was the women who had launched a massive movement against feudal and colonial rule.

Role vs. Status Paradox: Family vis-a-vis Social

We have seen above the significant and impactful role, women of Manipur have been playing in the socio-political sphere. It is incumbent on our part to examine their role and status at the micro level of the family. This would throw light on:

A. Whether there is a conflict or divergence in their role at the micro and the macro levels; and

B. Whether the significant social role they play is just an extension of the familial role or otherwise.

While attempting to answer these two questions, one is handicapped by the absence of data on family conditions of the period. Hence, one can only rely on the writings of the observers[41] of the contemporary social scene. This is exactly what is being adopted in this section.

One common strand emerges from the writings of these observers. They invariably noted the divergence of the women's familial and social status from the role they play at historically critical junctures. At the familial level, they found the wives purely subservient to the husbands; wives played very little, if any, role in the family decision-making process. While the role of women in the society insofar as it relates to the politico-administrative areas had been, as was seen above, very crucial, their overall status was in a way found to be not in keeping with their social role. In other words, the women seemed to play a very important role in the society seen as a collective of individuals, but when it came to society as an aggregate of families their status gets absolutely non-commensurate with their role. In still other words, there seems to be reversal of status as compared to the roles they play, which may be interpreted as a kind of paradox.

Now this seeming paradox needs an explanation. We had

stated passim that the primary objective of Manipuri women have been to ensure a stable and secured livelihood of the family. So long as they enjoyed an atmosphere for this, they were least bothered about anything else. But when they were pushed into conditions wherein such an atmosphere was jeopardised due to politico-administrative steps affecting mainly their men-folk, they would emerge as collective of women individuals and start revolting against the prevailing regime becoming a la tigress with the cubs.[42] There was thus an overall and temporal scenario of their status not being in tally with such discrete social uprisings of women. The final answer as to what was the facilitating factor enabling the women to play the active social role as and when needed by the society would require a separate study; we are yet to have an explanation of the invincibility of Manipuri women as collectives.[43]

Position of Women in Manipur after Colonial Rule

We have seen some critical developments relating to women during the Colonial period. First, the foundation for women's education was laid during this period. Secondly, women of Manipur collectively emerged as a very powerful socio-political force. Now it would be both relevant and interesting to examine how these developments impacted upon the post-colonial scenario. In the process, we can also study if there are any new dimension to the role and position of women in the post-colonial period.

Unlike the pre-colonial and colonial period a more systematic data about women are available for the post-colonial period. Accordingly, in what follows we shall be endeavouring to provide a picture of the developmental achievement of the women in this period through a set of indicators. This we do in two ways. First, we compare the indicators temporally by examining the changes in them in the terminal period as compared to those in the initial period. Secondly, we compare the position of women in Manipur with that of other provinces or the national average during the period under study.[44]

Population

Population of a country/state is its most important asset and resource for all kinds of development.[45] A glimpse of the distribution of the population of the State and All India by sex and decennial growth rate of the post-colonial period starting from 1951 to 2001, the latest year of census, is given in Table 2.9.

Table 2.9: Population of Manipur and All-India by Sex (1951-2001)

Year	*India*		*Manipur*		*Decennial Growth*	
	Male	*Female*	*Male*	*Female*	*India*	*Manipur*
1951	51.3	48.6	49.1	50.9	13.31	12.80
1961	51.5	48.4	49.6	50.4	21.64	35.04
1971	51.8	48.2	50.1	49.9	24.80	37.53
1981	51.7	48.3	50.7	49.3	24.66	32.46
1991	51.9	48.1	51.1	48.9	23.85	29.29
2001	51.7	48.3	50.6	49.4	21.56	24.86

Source: (a) *Census Publication of the Office of the Registrar General*, India.
(b) NEC, *Basic Statistics of the North Eastern Region* 2002, Shillong, 2004.

As seen from the table that the trend of equi-proportionality of the relative size of men and women is maintained right from the pre-colonial period till today in the State of Manipur.

Before analysing the overall population scenario, it would be appropriate to account for the low growth rate during 1941-51. The Census Report mentions that it was due to "devastation caused by the continued involvement of Manipur for long years in the World War II when it was occupied by the Japanese armies for quite some time in their advance from Burma towards India and the great shortage of medicine and supplies it gave rise to".[46]

When compared with the population growth rate of Manipur during the colonial period (Table 2.4), the post-colonial period depicts a higher growth rate. The decadal growth rate was 35.04 per cent during 1951-61, 37.53 per cent during 1961-71, 32.46 during 1971-81, 29.29 per cent during 1981-91 and 24.86 per cent during 1991-2001. Putting another way, the population growth rate in the post-colonial period peaked during 1961-71 while it has worn a declining trend after that. Decline in fertility has been identified as the main reason for the decline in the decadal growth rate. It needs especial mention here that Manipur's decadal growth rate has been higher than that of the national average throughout the period except during 1941-51.

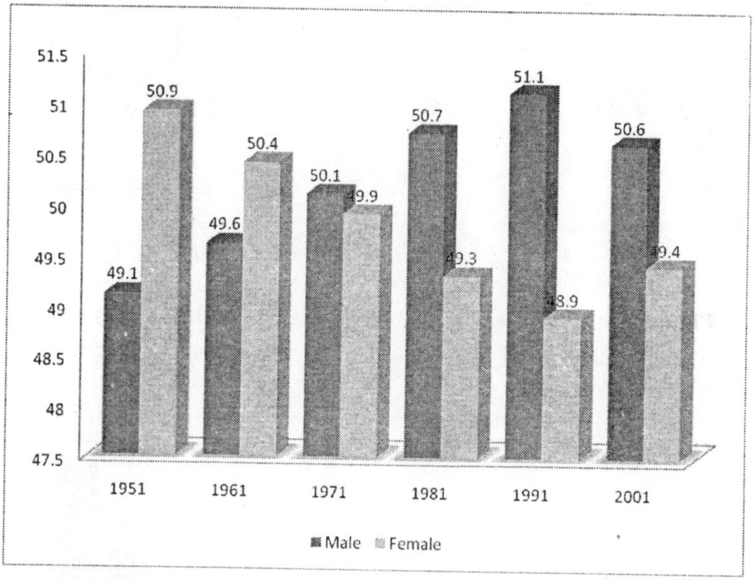

Figure 2.6: Sex Wise Population Growth of Manipur (1951-2001)

Figure 2.6 illustrate the sex-wise population growth of Manipur, 1951-2001. In addition, a diagrammatical representation of the decennial growth of Manipur and all-India is shown in Figure 2.7.

A combined picture of the female population growth rate for the period from 1881 to 2001 is given in Figure 2.8.

Sex Ratio (Females per thousand males)

It is pertinent to note that sex ratio is one of the important demographic indicators, and a closer balance between the sexes is globally accepted as a healthy sign of population situations. Table 2.10 presents the comparative figure of the sex ratio of Manipur and All India during the post-colonial period between 1951 and 2001, the latest year of Census data of which are available.

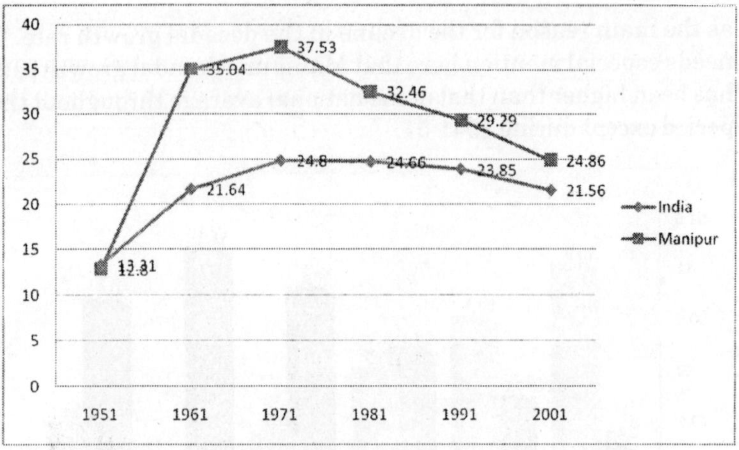

Figure 2.7: Decennial Growth of Manipur and All India (1951-2001)

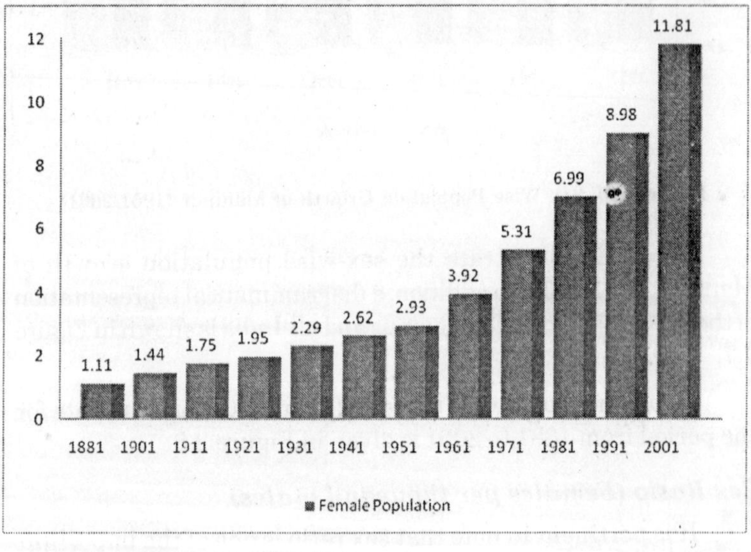

Figure 2.8: Female Population Growth of Manipur (1881-2001) (in lakhs)

Table 2.10: Sex Ratio of All-India and Manipur (1951-2001)

Year	*India*	*Manipur*
1951	946	1,036
1961	941	1,015
1971	930	980
1981	934	971
1991	927	958
2001	946	974

Source: (a) *Census Publication of the Office of the Registrar General*, India
(b) NEC, *Basic Statistics of the North Eastern Region 2002*, Shillong, 2004

It comes out glaringly from the table (Table 2.10) that the ratio has been lower at the national level than Manipur throughout the period under consideration. The Manipur scenario is particularly interesting. Though the ratio in Manipur has been higher than the national average all along, yet it shows a declining trend from 1961 to 1991. In 1961 the ratio was still in favour of women, starting as it were from a yet higher favourable situation in 1951.This favourable situation could, however, not be maintained, and the reversal started from the very next Census (1971). The unfavourable ratio still continues though in 2001 we observe a slight improvement in it. Research into this trend of sex ratio in Manipur would be important, but it is outside the scope of present book.

For the convenience of an overall comparison, the changing scenario of sex-ratio of Manipur for the entire period from 1881 to 2001 is shown in Figure 2.10. This figure is converted into a time-trend in Figure 2.11.

Literacy Rate

The level of literacy is one of the important factors with which we can judge the quality of population. Literacy and ipso facto education is given so much importance by contemporary researchers of development that it is now considered an

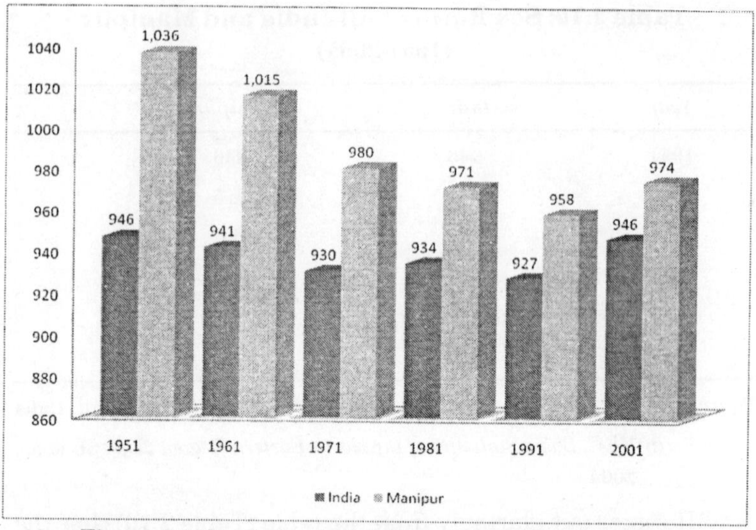

Figure 2.9: Sex Ratio of All-India and Manipur (1951-2001)

independent factor of production. In fact the resultant human capital is now at the core of growth theory.[47] Literacy is now considered as the surest means for emancipation from backwardness and poverty. Hence the importance is given today

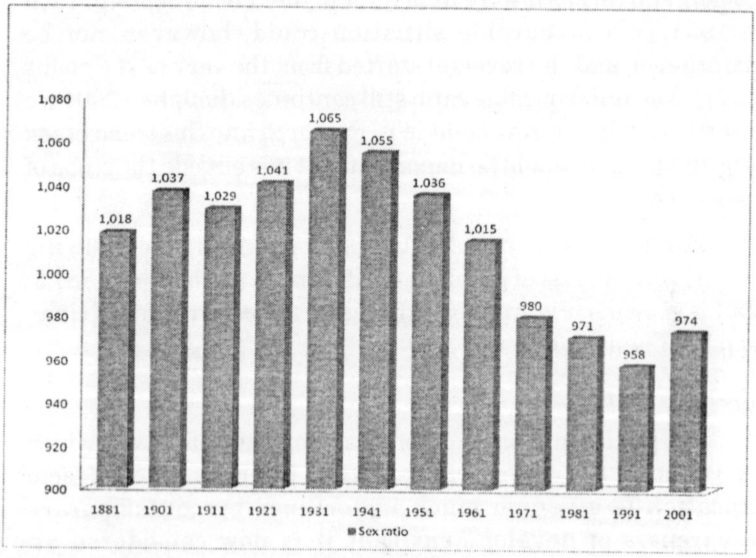

Figure 2.10: Sex Ratio of Manipur, 1881-2001

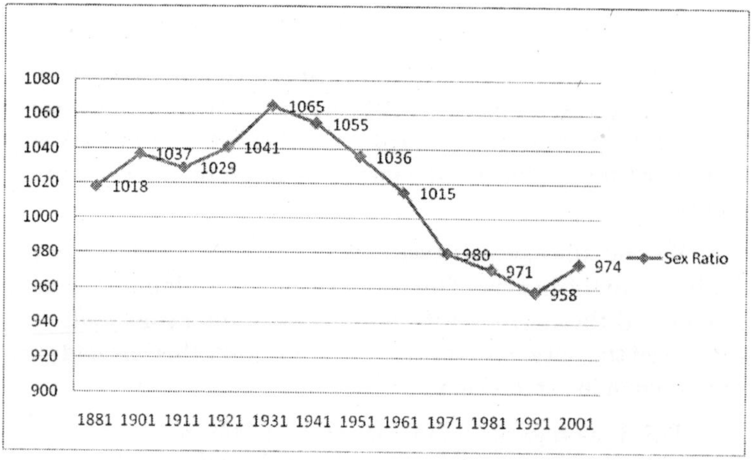

Figure 2.11: Sex Ratio of Manipur, 1881-2001

to higher literacy rates. Table 2.11 presents the male-female break up of literacy percentage of Manipur and all-India from 1951 to 2001.

Table 2.11: Literacy rate of Manipur and All-India by Sex (1951-2001)

Year	*Manipur*			*India*		
	Male	*Female*	*Total*	*Male*	*Female*	*Total*
1951	20.77	2.38	11.41	27.20	8.90	18.33
1961	45.12	15.93	30.42	40.40	15.40	28.30
1971	46.04	19.53	32.91	45.95	21.97	34.45
1981	53.29	29.06	41.35	56.3	29.7	41.44
1991	71.63	47.60	59.89	64.13	39.29	52.21
2001	80.30	60.60	70.50	75.85	54.1	64.2

Source: (a) *NEC, Basic Statistics of the North Eastern Region 2002*, Shillong, 2004

(b) *Economic Survey Manipur, 2002-2003*, Directorate of Economics and Statistics, Government of Manipur, p. 13

Note: Literacy rate is estimated on the basis of population aged 5 years and above in the Censuses of 1951, 1961 and 1971 while the population aged 7 years and above is accounted in the Censuses of 1981, 1991 and 2001.

The pictures emerging from the table are revealing:

First, we see that the literacy rate in Manipur has been on the continuously rising with 1951-61 as the decade of sharpest rise and it now stands at 70.50 per cent. This present literacy rate is higher than the national average by more than 6 percentage points.

Second, the period between 1951 and 1961 stands out as the landmark in the history of literacy movement in Manipur. During this period the literacy rate underwent a quantum jump and surpassed the national average. No period after this has had such a phenomenon expansion in literacy rate.

Third, as regards female literacy of Manipur, it has risen from 2.38 per cent in 1951 to 60.60 per cent in 2001[48] which implies a gain of more than 1 percentage point per year during the last fifty years as against 0.9 percentage point per year for all-India female literacy during the same period.

Table 2.11A: Gender Differential (Gap between Male and Female) in Literacy Rates by Manipur and All India, 1951-2001

(in percentage points)

Year	*Male Female Percentage Differential*	
	Manipur	*India*
1951	20.4	18.3
1961	35.75	25
1971	30.83	23.98
1981	27.66	26.6
1991	24.03	24.84
2001	19.7	21.75

Source: Computed from Table 2.10

Fourth, the scenario of male literacy rates always maintaining a lead over the female literacy rates during the colonial period is still continuing in the post-colonial period as well.[49]

Fifth, the male and female literacy rate differential in Manipur has declined from a differential of 36 percentage points in 1961 to one of about 20 percentage points in 2001. This is contrary to the scenario of colonial period when the differential disfavouring female kept on rising.[50]

Figure 2.12 shows a comparative picture of the gender differential in literacy rate by Manipur and India, 1951-2001.

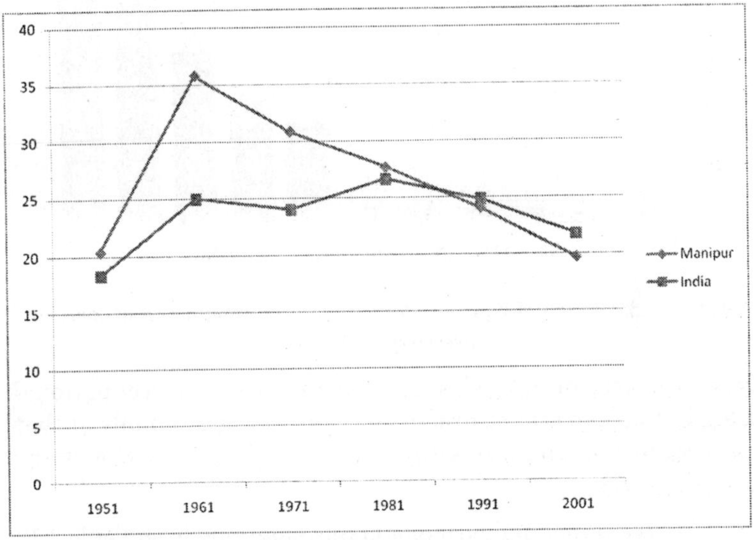

Figure 2.12: Gender Differential (Gap between Male and Female) in Literacy Rates by Manipur and All India, 1951-2001 (in percentage points)

The increasing trend of female literacy tates in Manipur for both the colonial and the post-colonial period is given in a graphic form in Figure 2.13.

Economic Status of Manipuri Women

The occupational structure of a State also signals the degree of structural change. In this section, we endeavour to provide an analysis of the occupational structure of the land. In Table 2.12, data relating to the distribution of population according to the three traditional sectoral classifications of Primary, Secondary and Tertiary are provided in the case of Main Workers. While interpreting the data, we should remember that the definition of a 'worker' has undergone changes in every Census of India.

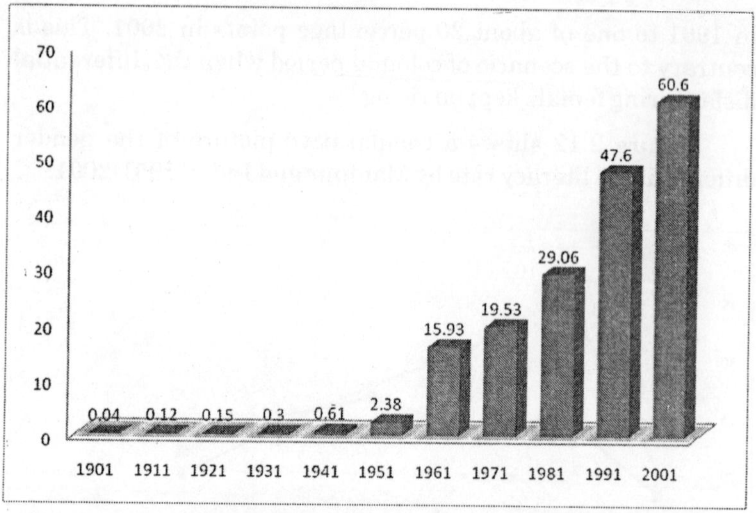

Figure 2.13: Growth of Female Literacy Rates of Manipur, 1901-2001 (in percentage points)

Nevertheless, broad inferences on the trend of occupational distribution can still be drawn, and more or less reliably at that for a State like Manipur with very little industrialisation if any over the years.

We are providing the major points emerging from Table 2.12 below.

First, it is seen from the table that Agriculture still constitutes, as in the colonial period, the sector wherein the largest proportion of women engage as do men. The latest Census of 2001 marks a landmark in the sense that the proportion of both men and women in agriculture experience a decline of about 18 percentage points and both reached a below 50 per cent mark.

Secondly, while the proportion of men in total men engaging in agriculture as the main occupation was higher than that of women during 1961 – 1981 though with decreasing margins. From the 1991 Census onwards we observe a reversal of this scenario with the female proportion of main workers in the total female workers surpassing that of male by over 7 percentage points in both 1991 and 2001 Censuses. In effect, we observe a trend of declining proportion of both male and female in the primary sector.

Table: 2.12: Distribution of Main Workers of Manipur by Main Industrial Categories and Sex (1961-2001)

(In percentages)

Industrial Category	*1961*		*1971*		*1981*		*1991*		*2001*	
	Male	*Female*	*Male*	*Female*	*Male*	*Female*	*Male*	*Female*	*Male*	*Female*
Primary sectors										
Cultivators	77.1	53.2	68.06	64.93	63.96	63.09	58.65	66.18	40.65	48.42
Agricultural Labourers	0.65	0.57	3.53	3.88	3.31	7.29	4.62	9.6	5.90	7.17
Fishing, Hunting, Livestock Plantation, Orchard & allied activities	0.31	0.13	0.83	0.22	1.45	0.31	2.09	0.69	-	-
Mining & Quarrying	-	-	0.03	0.01	0.04	0.03	0.04	0.02	-	-
Sub Total	78.06	53.90	72.45	69.04	68.76	70.72	65.40	76.49	46.55	55.59
Secondary Sectors										
Manufacturing, Processing, Servicing & Repairsa) Household Industry	3.98	41.12	2.4	22.91	2.01	20.17	1.45	11.95	3.33	12.58
b) Other than Household Industry	0.46	0.15	1.86	1.23	2.36	1.02	2.72	1.74	-	-
Construction	1.09	0.13	1.85	0.07	3.05	0.28	2.37	0.38	-	-
Sub Total	5.53	41.4	6.11	24.21	7.42	21.47	6.54	14.07	3.33	12.58

(contd.)

Table: 2.12 (Contd.)

(In percentages)

Industrial Category	*1961*		*1971*		*1981*		*1991*		*2001*	
	Male	*Female*	*Male*	*Female*	*Male*	*Female*	*Male*	*Female*	*Male*	*Female*
Tertiary Sectors										
Trade & Commerce	2.90	3.75	3.12	4.37	3.14	3.7	4.18	3.35	-	-
Transport, Storage and Communication	1.64	0.01	1.63	0.04	1.53	0.03	1.97	0.12	-	-
Other Services	11.85	0.92	16.69	2.33	19.15	4.06	21.91	5.97	50.05	31.83
Sub Total	16.39	4.68	21.44	6.74	23.82	7.79	28.06	9.44	50.05	31.83
Total	100	100	100	100	100	100	100	100	100	100

Source: *Census Publications of the office of the Registrar General*, India.

Note:
1. Figures shown in the category *Other Services* in the year 2001 refers to other workers i.e., those engaged in some economic activity during the last one year, but not as cultivators or agricultural labourers or manufacturing, processing, servicing and repairing in household industry.
2. Figures for 2001 exclude Mao-Maram, Paomata and Purul Sub-Division of Senapati District.

Third and an interesting picture emerging is the case of the decline in the primary sector proportions over the years not getting translated into a rise of the respective proportions in the secondary sector. This aspect particularly demands curiosity as Manipur happens to be a low industrialised State.

Fourth, when it comes to the secondary sector the true nature of productive activity other than agriculture occurring in the economy of Manipur comes out very well. For the economy as a whole, it speaks of the non-emergence of modern industrial activities, and the sustenance of the traditional non-farm activities singlehandedly by the womenfolk. This is the reason why the proportion of male in the total main male workers has remained below 10 per cent and still declining all through the period. But the heartening picture emerging in the case of secondary sector is the sharp decline of respective female proportions, with the high of 41.4 per cent in 1961 declining to only 12.58 per cent in 2001 – a slide of 0.72 percentage points every year over the period. This decline is sharpest in 1971 though this could be explained by the drastic change in the definition of 'worker' in the 1971 Census as compared to the previous ones. In the post-1971, the deepest decline in female proportions happened during 1971-1981.

Fifth, when it comes to the tertiary sector, the strange feature of Manipur's economy is the rising importance of this sector without ever passing through the phase of industrialisation unlike as had happened in the countries or regions now developed or developing. We must however hasten to add that the nature of tertiary activities now being witnessed in Manipur is very different from the one observed in other regions or countries. While what is being experienced in developed areas is the rising predominance of low-volume but high value activities with a significant value addition, the one Manipur is undergoing is one of low value, little value addition and very small scale activities.[51] Having mentioned something about the general picture, what is of relevance to the present study is the relative closing of gap by female workers in this sector. In 1961, the percentage of female main workers specialising in this sector's activities has risen by 6.8 times during 1961-2001, but this has been only 3.05 times in the case of male for the same period. In other words, the proportion of male was about 3.5 times of that of the female in 1961, but in 2001 it is now reduced to 1.57 times only. In still other words, while tertiary activities were mainly engaged by male, women are as well increasing opting for activities in this sector.

In the main, one sharp overall picture emerges from Table 2.12. It had been seen earlier the active engagement of women in various economic activities during the colonial period. Now in the post-colonial period too this trend continues with the female now challenging every bastion of male specialisation, e.g., the tertiary sector. To put it another way, there are elements of truth in the general parlance that the economy of the State is being sustained by the women. While the traditional productive activities are being sustained by the womenfolk, the increasing specialisation in new servicers sector as they relate to Manipur is observed more among women than among men.

For a better understanding, the proportion of women in total main workers in three different sectors i.e., primary, secondary and tertiary sectors from 1961 to 2001 are shown in Figure 2.14, Figure 2.15 and Figure 2.16 respectively.

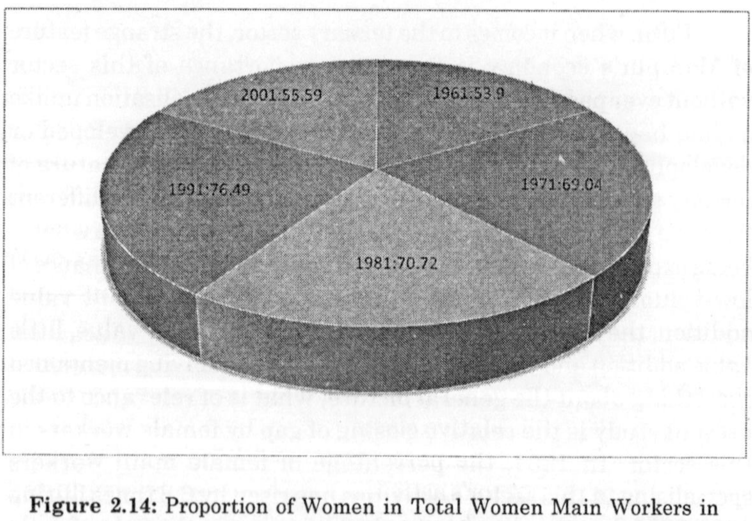

Figure 2.14: Proportion of Women in Total Women Main Workers in Primary Sector (1961-2001).

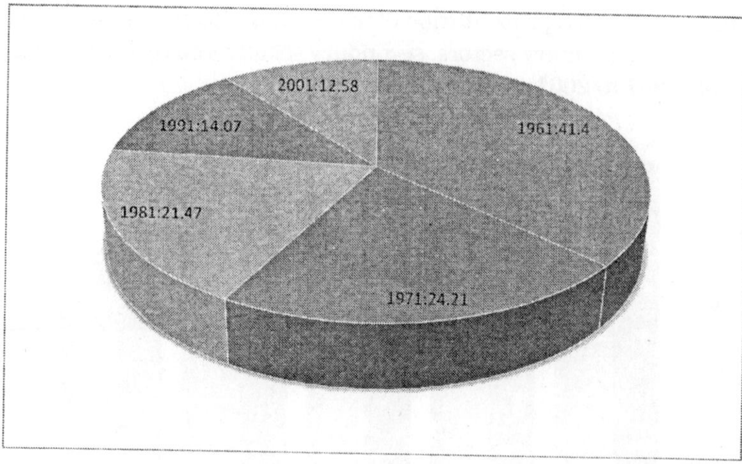

Figure 2.15: Proportion of Women in Total Women Main Workers in the Secondary Sector (1961-2001).

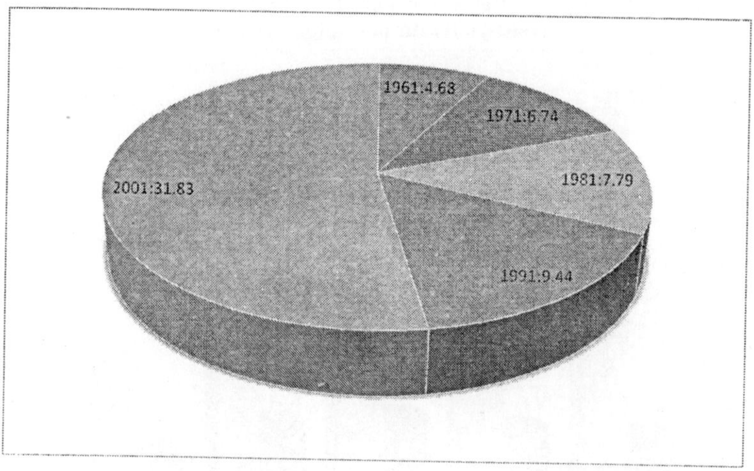

Figure 2.16: Proportion of Women in Total Women Main Workers in the Tertiary Sector (1961-2001).

Figure 2.17, Figure 2.18, and Figure 2.19 represents a diagrammatic representation of male-female distribution of main workers in primary sectors, secondary sectors and tertiary sectors from 1961 to 2001, respectively.

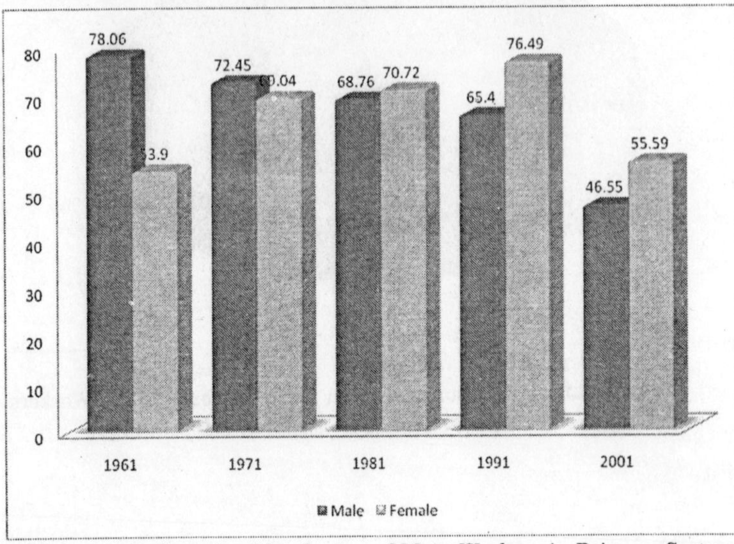

Figure 2.17: Sex-wise Distribution of Main Workers in Primary Sectors (1961-2001) (in percentage points)

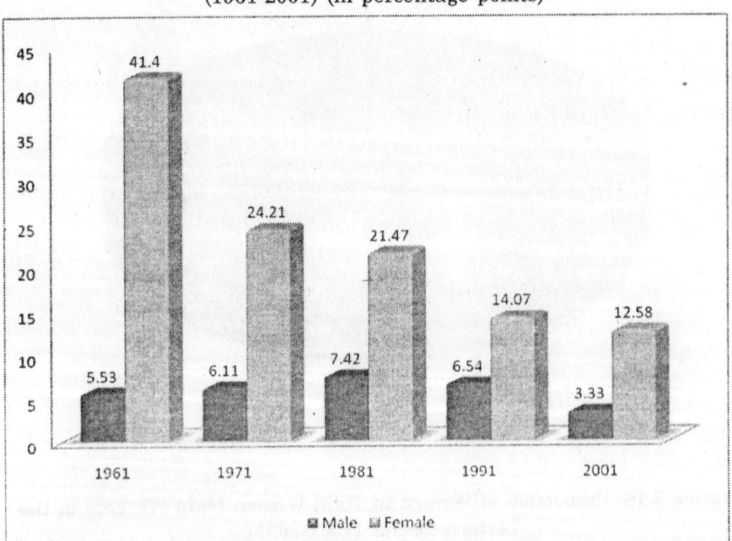

Figure 2.18: Sex-wise Distribution of Main Workers in Secondary Sectors (1961-2001) (in percentage points)

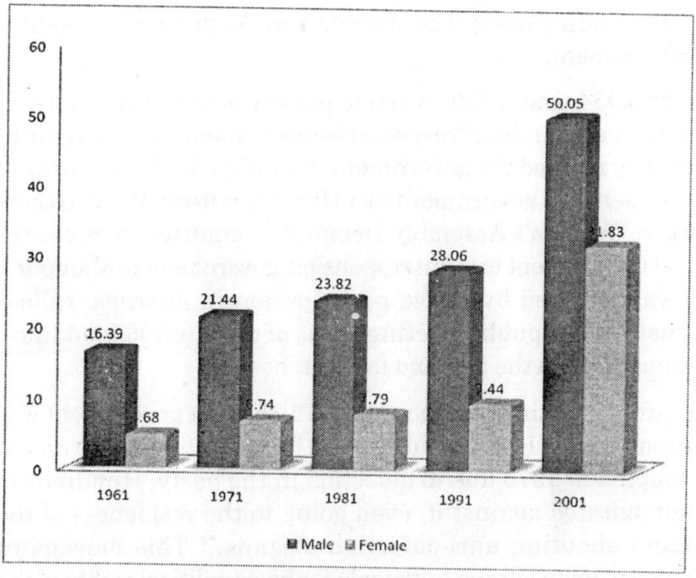

Figure 2.19: Sex-wise Distribution of Main Workers in Tertiary Sectors (1961-2001) (in percentage points)

A Noteworthy Trait of Manipuri Women: The Continuity

Women of Manipur, as we already know, played an active role in the historic mass movements against British colonial exploitation and feudal regimentation by the Maharaja. This being in the forefront in social movements has become as if an inherent tenet of women of Manipur. In the post-colonial period, the nature of social concerns has undergone a dramatic change, as it is wont in the context of changing social dynamics. But in these changed social milieu too the women of Manipur continue to play a leading and critical role in spearheading mass movements for realization of social goals. This is witnessed by various women's movements connected with the socio-political issues which are discussed below. No daily newspaper of the State is complete in this troubled State without some reports on women endeavouring for peace.[52]

Women in 1950s and 60s

In the 1950s and 1960s, there was a strong movement in Manipur called Statehood Movement wherein people of Manipur were demanding the status of a State on the principle of right to self-government.

In 1954 and 1959, women played active part in every movement demanding "responsible government" in Manipur by which they implied the government of a full-fledged State instead of the dependent government of a Union territory. In 1960 there emerged "Women's Assembly Demand Committee" to press the Central Government to grant responsible government to Manipur.[53] This was followed by active participation in dharnas, rallies, demonstrations, public meetings, etc., of the late 1960s adding a new dimension to the demand for Statehood.

After attaining Statehood in 1972, the first government was a coalition one led by Manipur Peoples Party. But this government was toppled in 1973 due to defection in the party. Hundreds of women agitated against it, even going to the residences of the defectors shouting anti-defection slogans.[54] This movement displayed women joining a struggle for basic political rights of the people and in a way foreshadowing the need for defectionless politics which India realised more than a decade later when the Anti-Defection Law was passed by Parliament in 1985 and with more stringent amendments later.

Women in 1970s

In the 1970s, people of Manipur started to witness an increasing phenomenon of alcoholism and its ill-effects in the society. At this critical juncture, women of Manipur rose to the occasion by launching the now famous *Nisha Bandh Movement*. Nisha means intoxication or an intoxicant whereas bandh denotes to stop or to prohibit. It was a movement launched to prohibit the production of the brew and punishing those who consume it.[55] Women in many localities formed themselves into small groups and gathered at vantage points in their own localities and maintained a night-long vigil to catch hold of the drunkards. They even organised meetings to create greater awareness about the harmful consequences of consuming intoxicants and also to secure support of the wider population for the movement. It was a spontaneous response by the womenfolk to a chronic social evil that was wrecking families economically. It is one of the best examples of a successful collective action in Manipur in particular and India in general in contemporary history.

Women in 1980s

One stark reality of Manipur at least during the last two or three decades has been the fight between the forces of the state and those of the non-state organisations looking for an alternative state. This naturally but unfortunately has claimed many lives without much accountability empowered the state forces are by the highly controversial Armed Forces Special Powers Act (Assam and Manipur), 1958.[56] This socio-historical juncture necessitated a kind of response to address the unprecedented social agonies. Again it was women who responded positively to the call of the times, particularly so in the light of their continuous historical capability for social movements. This was the moment when the earlier collective action of *Nisha Bandh* transformed itself into *Meira Paibi*[57] *Movement*. So the 1980s saw married women in the age group of 40-65 years keeping a night vigil of their respective localities with torches in their hands to thwart unwarranted and unexplained killing of youth by armed state forces. This signified an additional responsibility of womenfolk, protecting the innocent people from the harassment and killing by the state armed forces while still maintaining the movement against alcoholism.

These post-colonial movements of women speak volumes of the trajectory of their participation in socio-political issues. In earlier instances, their movement aimed at removing specific drawbacks of administrative or social functioning. But with the recent activism of the *Meira Paibis*, they have now emerged into active protagonists for a new social order.

Women in the New Millennium

The active involvement of women nurtured and perfected in the twentieth century continues to show its vibrancy in this millennium as well.[58] In June 2001, there was a mass movement in the State against the probable reduction in the territorial size of Manipur, in which women too did play their part. One recent internationally noted and impactful protest of women is the 2004 incident wherein women in nude displayed their anger by inviting the Armed Forces occupying the Kangla Fort[59] to come and rape them. The women went to this unique protest in the wake of the arrest, rape and brutal killing of a girl by the armed forces. The state security forces ultimately had to leave the Kangla.

Still another healthy and encompassing characteristic of the women's movement is the espousal of intercommunity bonds in these movements. Though the active participants have been mainly Meitei women, yet these have not necessarily implied confinement to the cause of Meitei people only. They have been forthcoming and staging protests if any gross injustice or violation of rights has been meted out to any other Manipuri or non-Manipuris staying in Manipur.

It would be incomplete to script the story of Manipur, more so with reference to contemporary Manipur, without a significant mention of an individual who has stood up against the power of an empire. Irom Chanu Sharmila has been struggling for peace and justice and courageously sacrificing for the highest good. She has been on protest fast unto death against the Armed Forces Special Power Act, 1958. She demonstrates in other words 'the power of the powerless'[60], linked, inextricably, to a collective aspiration.[61]

The upshot of the above discussions on the role and position of women in the socio-politico-economic fabric of the land lead us to an interesting paradox-like scenario. The participation of Manipuri women in modern formal political institutions has indeed been very marginal as was seen earlier. But on the other hand, we observe their confirmatory participation and impactful role in the informal manifestations of socio-political dynamics. Their role in the economic activities of the State has of course been exemplary. This paradoxical scenario needs active research, and as of now, some new unstructured debates have already started as to the status of Manipuri women. While the active involvement in the economic activities can be seen as the widening of the choice-set of women, which would be status enhancing, the non-translation of this into greater participation in formal political institutions can be interpreted as exploitation of women in guise of providing larger economic freedom. We can examine if this is another version of the informalisation of women's economic activities seen in India and the world as a whole.[62] It is found that 89 per cent in India and 94 per cent for the world as a whole, women work in the informal sector.

Conclusion

The geo-political location of Manipur at the intersection of South, South-east and East Asia has made it a melting pot of waves of people and their cultures. This necessarily has provided the women of the land with certain unique features. These features are rewarding areas for studies on women.

Some of these features have stood the test of history. Women of Manipur have been active in business related activities right from the pre-colonial to the post-colonial times of today. This has been coupled by the opportune and necessary involvements in movements for social, political and economic justice from time to time. The relative equi-proportionality of the size of men and women in the population has been a stable feature of the population right from the pre-colonial times. Though female literacy was understandably low in the beginning i.e., the end of the 19th century, it has been rising continuously though still below the male literacy rate. In fine, the confirmatory and the impactful role of women in the socio-politico-economic process of the State has been salient since long. The issue of concern, however, remains the lack of appropriate participation in formal political institutions, thereby raising the research question as to whether there is subordination of women in the guise of greater economic participation.

NOTES & REFERENCES

1. Lyall, A. in his introduction to Hodson, T.C., (1908), *The Meitheis*, David Nutt, London (Reprinted by Akansha, 2010), p. viii.
2. Dun, E.W., (1886), *Gazetteer of Manipur*, Reprinted by Vivek Publishing House, (1981), Delhi, p.17.
3. Grimwood, E.St.C., (1975), *My Three Years in Manipur*, Vivek Publishing House, Delhi, pp. 58-59.
4. Johnstone, J., (1987), *Manipur and the Naga Hills*, Gian Publishing House, New Delhi, pp. 134-135.
5. Barbara, W.E., ed., (1963), *Women in New Asia*, Amsterdam, p. 479.
6. Boserup, E., (1970), *Women's Role in Economic Development*, George Allen and Unwin, London,

7. Brown, R., (1975), *Statistical Account of Manipur*, first published in 1874, reprinted in 1975 by Sanskaran Prakashak, Delhi, p. 88

8. Dun, E.W., (1886), *op.cit.*, p. 26.

   This fear of the spread of education by the monarchy or a dictator is a fairly universal phenomenon. In this, one can see the characterization of the features of democracy and dictatorship as given in Daron, A., and Robinson, J., (2006), *Economic Origins of Dictatorship and Democracy*, Cambridge University Press, New York. While citing this reference, no inference is being made about the form of Government which prevailed in Manipur.

9 Even in India, which has a long history of institutionalized education dating back to the first millennium, female education was partially recognized by the Government as a branch of state system of education only in 1854. See for example Mukerji, S.N., (1961), *History of Education in India*, Baroda, p.120, Naik, J.P. and Syed, N. (1974), *A Students History of Education in India (1800-1974)*, Delhi, p.47, 55.

10. Shakespear, J., (1907), *Manipur under British Management 1891-1907*, Shillong, p. 7.

11. Devi, J., (1989), *Education in Manipur*, Rai Pravina Brothers, Imphal, p. 37.

12. Shakespear, J., *op.cit.*, p. 5.

13. While examining the position of women in the economy and society of Manipur, it would be relevant to recall here that one should not be looking at it from the perspective of the realities being faced in the other parts of the country for the societal context is vastly different in the State. For an appreciation of the overall Indian scenario, see, *World Economic Forum*, (2009), *The India Gender Gap Review* 2009, Geneva.

14. All Occupations were divided into 6 classes, 18 Orders and 75 Sub-orders. The 6 Classes and 18 Orders adopted are listed below: A. Professional Class: i) Persons engaged in the general or local Government of the Country; ii) Persons engaged in defences of Country; and iii) Persons engaged in learned professions or in Literature, Art and Science (with their immediate Subordinate).

B. The Domestic Class: i) Wives; and ii) Persons engaged in entertaining and performing personal offices for men.

C. The Commercial Class: i) Persons who buy or sell, keep or lend money, houses or goods of various kinds; and ii) Persons engaged in conveyance of men, animals, goods, messages.

D. The Agricultural Class: i) Persons possessing or working on the land and engaged in growing grain, fruit, grasses, animals and other products; and ii) Persons engaged about animals.

E. Industrial Class: i) Persons engaged in arts and mechanic productions; ii) Persons working and dealing in textile fabrics and in dress; iii) Persons working and dealing in food and drinks; iv) Persons working and dealing in animal substance; v) Persons working and dealing in vegetable substance; and vi) Persons working and dealing in minerals.

F. The Indefinite and Non-Productive Class: i) Labourers and Others; ii) Persons of rank and property not returned under any occupation; and iii) Persons of no specified occupations. The above information is taken from Census of India, 1971.

15. This is borne by both legendary and historical evidences. The legendary Laisana, queen of the First King of Manipur, Nongda Lairen Pakhangba, after the death of her husband, continued to rule for the safeguard of the motherland. See *Cheitharol Kumbaba*, (1967), Imphal, p.48. Cf. Branisa, B., Klasen, S., Ziegler, M., (2009), Why we should all Care about Social Institutions related to Gender Inequality, Discussion Paper No. 15, Courant Research Centre, Gottingen University, October.

16. Dun, E.W., (1886), *op.cit.*, p. 17.

17. *Ibid.*

18. Murthi, R.K. (1984), "Daring Dames of Manipur", in Ahluwalia, B. K., and Ahluwalia, S., *op.cit.*, p. 73.

19. Cf. Boserup, E., (1970), *op.cit.*, p. 16.

20. Sircar, M. Chaki, (1984), Chapter 4 in *Feminism in a Traditional Society: Women of Manipur Valley*, Vikas Publishing House, Delhi, p. 38.

21. Gupta, M., (2000), "Indicators of Women Development", Chapter 11 in Gupta, M. (2000), ed., *Economic Participation of Women*, Vol.1, Sarup and Sons, New Delhi, p.146.

22. *Lallup* was a feudal service rendered by an adult subject to the king for ten days out of every forty. The service might be in the form of military duties or development work like the construction of roads and bridges or working in the king's estate, etc. And those who rendered *Lallup* service did not pay any revenue.

23. This view gets reflected in the archival materials. The same opinion is held strongly by scholars working in this area and personally interviewed specifically for the present research work.

24. Queen Linthoingambi is still remembered for her presence of mind and courage while dealing with the Tangkhul tribes during the absence of the king Ningthoukhomba (1432-1467). (N. Khelchandra, *Thangmeiron,* unpublished, p. 7).

25 Dun, *op. cit.,* passim.There are scholars who maintain that the exercise of powers of administration by the British was de jure as the degree of intervention in the administration of Manipur by the Britishers underwent a sharp increase. See, in this connection, Sharma, H. Dwijasekhar and A. Brajakumar Sharma, "Economic history of Manipur during the British Raj", in Sharma, H. Dwijasekhar (2009), ed., *New Insights into the Glorious Heritage of Manipur*, Vol. 3, Akansha, New Delhi, Chapter 11. But we would prefer the de facto term as the traditional institutions like king were still maintained even after 1891, though the control over the administration by the Britishers did become conspicuous.

26. Mullan, C.S., (1932), *Census of India*, 1931-Vol. III-Assam-Part I, Report, p.29. The influenza epidemic was a more or less global disaster while the Kuki rebellion was a rebellion by the Kukis against the forced recruitment of Kukis by the Britishers for emigration to Mesopotamia as labourers.

27. The Census enumerations of the population of Manipur in 1872 and 1881 were not exhaustive and well organized. Again, the census enumeration papers for 1891 were destroyed during Anglo-Manipur War that year. Therefore, we shall use the Census Reports from 1901 onwards for reviewing the progress of literacy of the people of Manipur. See, *Census Report*, 1901.

28. In this connection, please refer to Section 2.2.2 above, which discussed the growth of modern education in Manipur.

29. It was because of this taboo that weaving and spinning were added to the curriculum to attract females to the schools. See Devi, J., *op. cit.*, p. 35, 36.

30. It might be mentioned here that the occupational classifications given in the censuses are more than twenty under eight main categories, but for purposes of analytical convenience we have adopted the grouping into five categories given by Ganguly, J. B., *op.cit.*, p. 371.

31. Allen, B.C., (1901), *Census of India*,Vol. IV, Assam Part I, Report, p.162.

32. "Manipuri women did produce some quantities of textile fabrics for sale no doubt and many of them were also traders who dealt in both agricultural produce as well as textiles. Therefore the low proportion of commercial population should be ascribed to an under-enumeration". *Ibid.*, p.168.

33. The information on economic activity of the individual was collected since 1872 Census. From 1901 to 1921, information on principal and subsidiary occupation or means of subsistence of actual workers was recorded. The term actual worker also included persons who were in receipt of income without doing work such as rentiers and pensioners etc. In 1931 Census, the term 'actual worker' was replaced by the earner. The population was classified into earners, working dependents and non-working dependents. See Census 1951.

34. Murthi, R.K., *op cit.*, p.74.

35. File No. XXXIV, Office of the Political Agent in Manipur, (Nupilal-1904), Secretariat Library, Imphal, p.4.

36. Constantine, R. (1981), *Manipur: Maid of the Mountains*, Lancers Publication, New Delhi, p.138.

37. Singh, J. Naorem, (1991), "Anti-British Movement: 1904-1949", in Dena, L., (1991), ed., *History of Modern Manipur: 1826-1949*, Orient Publishers, New Delhi, pp. 122-123.

38. *Administrative Report of Manipur Political Agency (1939-1940)*, p.1

39. Courtesy: *Poknapham*, a local daily, 12th December, 2007 made available to me by Maniton of HERICOUN (Ethno Heritage Council, Manipur).

40. A more or less similar characteristic of women emerging into active socio-political involvement in a context of political and administrative turmoil has also been reported in the larger South-east Asian context. See, Chaudhuri, S., (2010), *Women's Empowerment in South Asia and Southeast Asia: A Comparative Analysis*, MPRA Paper No. 19686.

41. (a) Brown, R., *op. cit.*, pp.71.

(b) Raghumani, S., (1988), "Meitei Personal Law", in Sanajaoba, N., (1988), *Manipur: Past and Present*, Mittal Publications, Delhi, pp. 341.

(c) Devi, B. Kshetrimayum, (1988), "Manipuri Women – A Study", in Sanajaoba, N., *op. cit.*, pp. 162, 168.

42. It was mentioned earlier the basic capability of Manipuri women to identify strongly with whatever they are associated with. This must be true whether it comes to husbands, children, family or society.

43. It could be the one mentioned earlier wherein there is no tradition in the State of women being locked inside the house. Whether this was because of the women having attained a certain voice or because the men found the situation more convenient to them or still a concatenation of these two factors remains to be enquired. It could as well be the behavioural perspective of Manipuri women stand out for the sake of survival of the family when any economic crisis befell the family and when the male breadwinner model breaks down. In such a crucial situation, they never think about their superior or inferior position, and their mind and energy is heavily betrothed for the welfare of the family.

44. Yumnam, A.(2005), "Development Experience of Manipur: A Framework for Industrialization" in Das, G., (2005), ed., *Structural Change and Strategy of Development, Resource-Industry Linkages in North-East India*, Akansha Publishing House, New Delhi, p. 83.

45. Simon, J. (1981), *The Ultimate Resource*, Princeton, Princeton University Press.

46. Vaghaiwalla, R.B., (1951), *Census of India*, Volume XII, Assam, Manipur and Tripura, Part I-A, Report, p.39.

47. See for instance, Lucas, R. (1988), "On the mechanics of economic development", *Journal of Monetary Economics*, Vol-22, p. 3-42.

48. As per 2001 Census, Manipur rank 20th in the State-wise Female-Literacy Rate while Kerala ranks 1st with 87.86% and Bihar placing last with 33.57%.

49. Please refer Table 2.7 B and Table 2.11.

50. See Table 2.7B (i).

51. The prominent examples are the Pan kiosks and tea stalls.

52. For example a recent headline of leading English daily, *The Sangai Express*, reports on a movement by women in its 16 June 2009 edition thus: Campaign against violence kicks off.

53. Bimola, Ksh., *op cit.*, pp. 168-169.

54. Statement of the All Manipur Statehood Demand Committee, *Anouba Samaj*, a local daily, Imphal 18th September 1968, p.3.

55. For further detail please refer Devi, J., (1999), "Women's Movement in Manipur—Past and Present", in *Manipur Today*, DIPR, Government of Manipur, Imphal, 26th January, p.14.

56. Under this Act, the state armed forces can kill anyone on suspicion and there can be no legal remedy for the victim.

57. *Meira* means Torch and *Paibi* means Bearer.

58. Refer footnote 52 above. Also note the spontaneous as well as instantaneous call for a twenty four hours bandh in Manipur by the various bodies of the women vendors consequent upon the killing of a pregnant mother in her another child's presence and expressing anguish and disapproval of the act. This happened during the peak hours of business in Imphal city on 23 July 2009. A leading daily runs the banner thus: "Women Vendors call 24 hrs bandh", *The Sangai Express*, Imphal, 24 July 2009. The same daily also reports on a movement by these women vendors in its 25 July 2009 edition thus: Resign: Women bodies to MLAs.

59. The original site of coronation of Kings and palace in Manipur.

60. This term was originally used by Victor Havel in connection with the Burmese democratic movement leader Aung San Suu Kyi, and it implies the invincible force of millions of people, who seek to live in peace. This is as quoted by Mehrotra, D. Priya, (2009), *Burning Bright: Irom Sharmila and the Struggle for Peace in Manipur*, Penguin Books, India, pp.167.

61. November 2, 2000, marked the death of ten innocent people, all killed when some Assam Rifles personnel opened indiscriminate firing under the immunity granted by the Armed Forces Special Power Act. The blood of ten innocent people, however, did not go in vain, for it gave birth to the crusader in Irom Chanu Sharmila. With an inner strength, she took the unilateral decision to sit on fast from November 5, 2000, until the Armed Forces Special Power Act is removed. *ibid.*

62. See Azad, N., (2007), "Towards an Engendered Poverty Paradigm in SAARC", in Arunachalam, J., and Kalpagam, U.,(2007), ed., *Rural Women in South Asia*, Rawat Publications, Jaipur, India, p. 274.

3

Women in Market

Introduction

In the earlier chapters, particularly the immediate previous chapter, we have seen a broad picture of the role and status of Manipuri women in the socio-politico-economic fabric of the land starting from the colonial period to till date. In the process, we have seen that the economic role of them has been dominantly tremendous over the centuries. We have as well seen that their informal civil sector engagement in socio-political issues has been confirmatory and impactful in every epoch of history. The paradoxical nature when they are conspicuously absent in the sphere of formal political processes and bodies has also been noted.

In this and the following chapters, we shall be endeavouring to re-examine the macro view from the micro perspective. We shall be doing so by delving into the role, status and functionings of the women in the Khwairamband Keithel, the historic market which has been the domain of purely of women traders all throughout. In order to facilitate this micro examination of women issues through the prism of participants in this market place, we start with a brief conceptual exposition of the market, followed by a picture of the location, origin and the present socio-economic characteristics of the vendors in this market place. This way we shall endeavour to look into the micro foundations of the women's role, status and functionings in Manipur.

Concept of Market

With the increasing degree of sophistication of the economy, the importance of market keeps on rising since market has been reasonably defined as an institution where willing buyers meet willing sellers through the mechanism of price. The vast array of available commodities is, in a way, the foundation of market while the buyers and sellers are players of market. The market players cannot participate in the game of marketing in the absence of competing commodities or complimentary commodities. Hence other things remaining the same, the principle of substitution and the principle of complimentarity constitute the crux of the issue.[1]

Being the link between the buyers and the sellers, market is naturally the connecting bridge between production and consumption. "Market" refers to a place or locality where a commodity or commodities are bought and sold. The product of a market may be local, national or international. However, in economics, the term market does not refer to a particular place in which things are bought and sold but to the whole of any region where buyers and sellers transact business for the exchange of particular goods and services and where the prices for these goods and services tend towards equality.[2]

Origin of Market Centres and Marketing

Thus spatial linkages emerged through the process of movement of products from the producer to the consumer. Study of this emergence is significant in every social context. And so is the case in the present context as well.

Starting from the earliest system of exchange in the form of silent barter, the market has travelled a long way in its evolutionary process depending on the emergence of new economic activities and the process of social evolution. The origin and development of marketing and market places are closely associated with development of man's activity or in other words with the history of civilization. Simple, unorganized and rudimentary trade or exchange of commodities is as old as man's society. To begin with, there was silent barter. Under it, one would leave his product at some selected place, while the person who required that article also do so and wait for some time. If the first person took away the offering, it meant that the offer had been accepted. Later on barter system became common and was in practice even after the development of coins as medium of exchange. This system was prevalent in many parts of India as well as in the State Manipur.

Although, the earliest man believed in self-sufficiency and had no idea either of exchange or trade, his very limited wants were satisfied by his immediate environment or by the place he used to move in search of food, water, favourable climate, etc. or remained unfulfilled. This nomadic culture too had occasional free exchange of gifts or reciprocal exchange of needed items. With the growth of social contacts and when man started living in groups, he began the practice of exchange of commodities.[3] "Accidental surpluses, specialization of production, presence of a rare and desirable item, or the need of essential products, gave rise to the exchange of goods which, in turn made man enlarge his knowledge of goods and his desire to obtain them".[4] As Hodder[5] explained, evolution of market starts from individual self-sufficiency to barter, followed by periodic assembly of buyers and sellers and finally establishment of permanent shops and markets as well as the start of daily and long distance trading. This contrasts with the view of others who opine that market centres are the result of long distance trading in order to fulfil the demands of a region.[6]

While the examination of how markets and market places have evolved in Manipur relative to the global experience would be more interesting and rewarding, it is well beyond the scope of the present book. However, an examination of the role of the market is paramount within the context of the present research. Hence, in what follows we examine the role the market has been playing in the socio-politico-economic milieu of Manipur.

Role of the Market and Marketing

The market has a unique role to play. In an economy where resources are at the hands of private individuals, profit motive and self-interests guide production activities and, as Adam Smith argue, social benefits are automatically maximised. This is to say that the market provides the incentives to economic growth. The importance of the market is being reappreciated all over again after the collapse of the communist bloc of countries, and a new political economy is in resurgence.[7]

In fact, the role of the market is now expanded to cover many social functions as well. For instance, marketing nowadays in its developmental sense is expected to educate people, cultivate changes in public attitude, spread civilisation and improve the quality of life.[8] Further, it strives to build efficient economic and social institutions and ensures satisfaction of the people who are the primary beneficiaries of the national development. Thus, in a developmental sense markets have assumed a significant place in the society and contribute to the economic upliftment of the people whom they serve.

It is this developmental perspective of market that we shall be adopting in this book.

Role of Market in Manipur

The Manipuri society is in the midst of rapid social change, which is visualized in the form of changing habits, customs, behaviour and attitude of the people. Markets in Manipur, as elsewhere though with unique local characteristics, are one of the most important institutions of social change and centres to disseminate new ideas and spread civilization. Markets in Manipur may also be considered as the nerve centres of socio-economic activities of the State. The role played by the market, as manifested through the participants in the market, in bringing about social change in the Manipuri society cannot be lost sight of.

Sanakeithel (Khwairamband Keithel) as a Marketing Centre

Imphal, the capital town of Manipur, is the nerve centre of the major social, economic and religious activities. Being the administrative capital of the State as well, it is also the core arena of political activities.

The Khwairamband Bazaar popularly known as Sanakeithel (*Sana*-golden, *Keithel*-market) is located at the centre of Imphal. A market centre with deep historical roots, it is the largest shopping centre, exclusively run by women, for artistic, exquisite, world famed Manipuri handloom and handicrafts. Moreover, it is also a place where women traders transact the business of local agricultural produce and other essential commodities. Women commuters from different places come to the daily bazaar to participate in the commercial transactions of various kinds. This Sanakeithel is no less an active centre of social gatherings than a vibrant economic place. Different kinds of women's activities such as political and social, other than economic and commercial activities, are also being continuously carried out at this place by the women traders. This market centre is supposed to be the biggest women's market in Asia in terms of the number of women participating in it.

Beauty of the Khwairamband Keithel

Contemporary women scholars are particularly overwhelmed by not only the aesthetic value of this market but also by the deeper socio-politico implications of it. "It looks surrealistic, like a painting, as the women vendors mostly Meitei, are beautiful with the white lines of a tilak on their forehead, shiny hair in buns, there is a sense of power, and that too from women's solidarity, flowing from their persona. No noise here of shouting, calling of shoppers, or the bustle of bargaining. There is a dignity, an aura radiated by strong, self-assured women".[9] With all the dynamics of hectic business of a thriving market, and women vendors' gossip, giggle and singing, which create a natural aura of relaxation, this market place is sacred to the women traders of Manipur in particular and to the women of Manipur in general for it gives strength and inspiration to them.

Contemporary Scenario

Given the above background, we now come to the analysis of role and position of women vendors in this market on the basis of survey specifically conducted for the purpose. The survey period extended over two months.[10]

While details of the market and the survey have been given in Chapter 1, before we come to the analysis of the market on the basis of the survey we highlight some prominent features immediately salient in the market. First, it relates to business practices. A variety of weights and measures are used in this market ranging from use of weighing machines to selling through approximation. Standard weights and measures like gram and kilogram are also used for various items of sale. Some vegetables, fish, channa (gram), and fruits vendors sell their products through approximation. Cloths are measured by human arm besides the standard measurement in meters. Standard weights and measures are largely used for the sale of fish, and rice and a few for vegetables and fruits.

The second one relates to mode of exchange. As understandable, much of the exchange during the kings' rule was based on the barter system. But this has now undergone a significant change. It is now fully monetised.[11]

The Survey

For the purpose of clarity and proper appreciation of the findings, it is incumbent on our part to explain at this stage the instrument of the survey. The survey was conducted with the help of a structured questionnaire, which contained 69 questions.[12]

The questions were framed in order to capture all the information relevant for the research. We start with the necessity of situating the women vendors in their socio-economic and household background. So the Questions 1 to 7 are meant to establish the socio-economic and spatial background of the interviewees. From this we proceed to collect information which reflects the dynamics of the market and relationships with the market of the women vendors. This section constitutes the core of the survey, and hence it contains the largest number of questions. Questions 8 to 54 form this section. The participation in the market and involvement in the socio-politico-economic dynamics caused by the market cannot be without impact on the traditional familial relationships and responsibilities of the women. We endeavour to extract information on this score through Questions 55 to 64. The remaining questions (five in all) are meant to identify the driving force and social alertness of the women vendors.

In the light of the above background, we now provide in what follows a picture of the women vending in Khwairamband Keithel.

A Profile of Women Vending in Khwairamband Keithel

Age

For our analysis, we have classified the vendors into seven categories of age groups ranging from 25 to 85 plus years of age; the age range for each group adopted for the analysis is ten years. A picture of the age distribution is given in Table 3.1.

Table 3.1: Age Distribution of Women Vendors

Category	*Age (in years)*	*Number*	*Percentage Distribution*
I	25 – 34	6	2.00
II	35 – 44	43	14.33
III	45 – 54	87	29.00
IV	55 – 64	95	31.67
V	65 – 74	57	19.00
VI	75 – 84	10	3.33
VII	85 +	2	0.67
	Total	300	100

Source: Personal Survey.

The relative shares of the different age groups as evinced indicate the following:

A. One very striking feature emerging from the table is the presence of very elderly women (75 years and above) in the market. They constitute almost 4 per cent of the total women vendors. It could be that these women just do not have other members of their family who could take on their business or plain used to participating in the market. The picture would be clear as we proceed in our analysis.

B. Another striking feature is the pre-eminence of the women of the ages between 45 and 64. The two age groups of 45-54 and 55-64 together constitute a whopping 60 per cent of the total women vendors. If we add to this the proportion of the women in the ages between 65 and 74, the share becomes almost 80 per cent of the total. Given the fact that this age range would be one with the maximum liability for family expenses as it would generally coincide with their children either maturing (whether after completion of education and training or not) or just matured and ready to settle down for their own life, the implications are many. We would come to these when we analyse the other economic issues relating women to the market.

C. In a way reminding of the household economic responsibilities of women, the active involvement of women in the market starts from the age group of 35-44, the age group for whom the children would be growing up and start needing funds for their educational and other developmental interventions. The proportion of this age group in the total of women vendors rises as high as 14 per cent from the low of 2 per cent of the age group just lower, 25-34.

The age distribution of women vendors is shown in Figure 3.1.

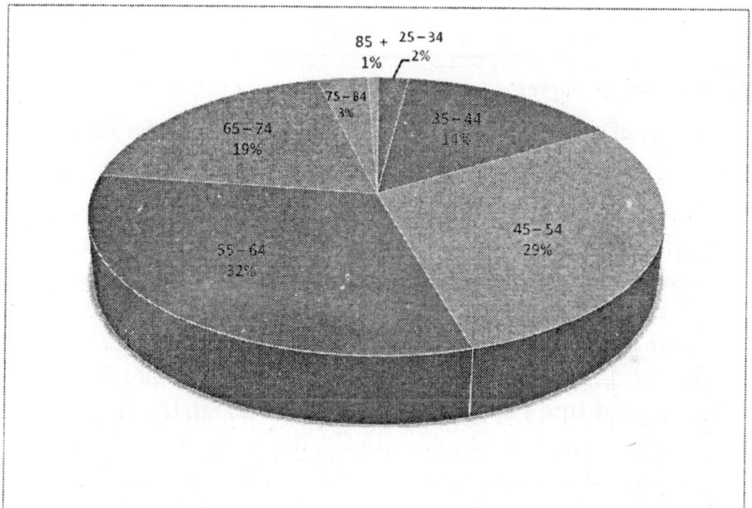

Figure 3.1: Age Distribution of Women Vendors

Educational level

We classify the educational level of women vendors into six categories as I. Illiterates; II. Below Matriculation; III. Matriculates; IV. Intermediates; V. Graduates; and VI. Above Graduates. The distribution of women according to educational qualification is given in Table 3.2.

Table 3.2: Distribution of Women Vendors by Educational Level

Category	*Education*	*Number*	*Percentage Distribution*
I	Illiterates	50	16.67
II	Below Matriculate	165	55.00
III	Matriculates	58	19.33
IV	Intermediates	21	7.00
V	Graduates	5	1.67
VI	Above	1	0.33
	Total	300	100

Source: *Personal Survey*

Some of the prominent pictures emerging from the Table 3.2 are:

A. The literacy rate among the women vendors is significantly high with as much as more than 80 per cent (83.33%) having attended educational institutes and acquired certain minimum educational qualifications. Of these the highest proportion is of the Below Matriculates constituting almost 55 per cent of the total. Together with the Matriculates (19.33 per cent), they constitute 74 per cent of the total. Though the proportion is small, there are women with Graduate and Post-Graduate qualifications participating in this market. The implication of this could be that those with Graduate and Post-Graduate Degrees would find it easier to find a placement in the job market elsewhere while the Matriculates and below find it rather difficult. It could also be because of the low proportion of women with these qualifications in the general population as well.

B. A cross examination of the literacy figures with the age information of the respondents, it comes out that none of women above the age of 69 was literate. It as well comes out that the literacy level rises as we go down the age ladder; the younger women have generally higher educational levels. The percentage distribution of women vendors by educational level is shown in Figure 3.2.

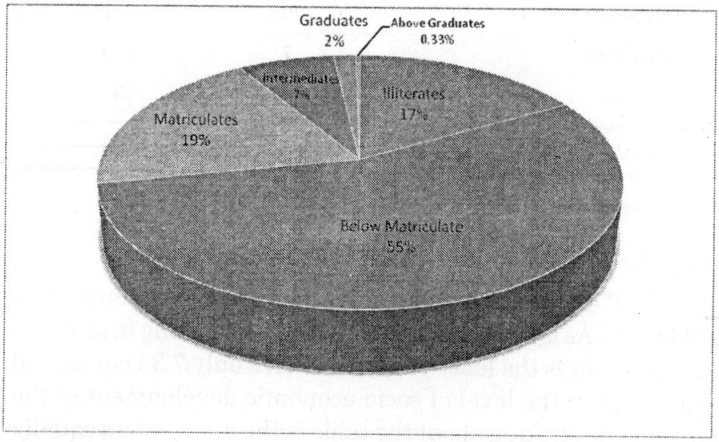

Figure 3.2: Percentage Distribution of Women Vendors by Educational Level

Marital Status

A picture of the marital status of the women vendors is given in Table 3.3. It is clear from the table that most of the women in the market are married; 69.33 per cent are currently married, 2.34 per cent divorcees, and 28 per cent are widows; these together constitute 99.67 per cent of the total. The high proportion of widows at 28 per cent of the total speaks of the economic and familial compulsions under which they might be functioning. Even in normal circumstances characterising a growing economy, widows do face a less friendly environment than other individuals. But the overall situation in Manipur has been much grimier from at least two angles. First, the economy of Manipur has not been one featuring expanding employment opportunities. Secondly, the overall socio-politico scenario of Manipur over the last three decades or so has been marked by unprecedented turmoil. These situations would naturally compound the challenges and difficulties that widows would face.

Table 3.3: Marital Status Distribution of Women Vendor

Category	*Marital Status*	*Number*	*Percentage Distribution*
I	Unmarried	1	0.33
II	Married	208	69.33
III	Divorcee	7	2.34
IV	Widow	84	28
	Total	300	100

Source: Personal Survey

Type of the Family

Table 3.4 gives a picture of the distribution of vendors by type of family. As is evident from the table vendor living in separate family constitutes the least proportion with only 7.33 per cent of the total. Given the level of socio-economic development of the region, what is striking about the table is the more or less equally high proportion of vendors from joint and nuclear families.[13]

Table 3.4: Distribution of Vendors by Type of Family

Category	*Type of the family*	*Number*	*Percentage Distribution*
I	Separate	22	7.33
II	Joint	145	48.33
III	Nuclear	133	44.33
	Total	300	100

Notes: Nuclear family- Living with parents and children. Joint family- Living with parents, sons, daughters, in-laws and grandchildren. Separate family- Living with in-laws, children.

Size of the Family

We have divided the family size into three categories: A. Single Family – as the name implies a single individual family either due to death of husband or divorce, or the children having all got married and maintaining separate household; B. Small

Family – a family with only one or two children; and C. Large Family – a family with more than two children, or living jointly with uncle, aunt and in-laws.

A picture of the distribution of the women vendors by family sizes is given in Table 3.5. As is clear from the table, Single Family vendors constitute at only 1 per cent a very small proportion of the total. The largest proportion of the women belong to Large Families (57 per cent), followed not far behind by those belonging to Small Families (42 per cent).

Table 3.5: Distribution of Vendors by Size of Family

Category	*Size of family*	*Number*	*Percentage Distribution*
I	Single member	3	1
II	Small Family	126	42
III	Large Family	171	57
	Total	300	100

Source: *Personal Survey*

Note: *Single family*: A single individual family either due to death of husband or divorce, or the children having all got married and maintaining separate household.

Small family: A family having only one or two children.

Large family: A family having more than two children or who live jointly with uncle, aunt or in-laws.

District and Religion

In Table 3.6 a picture of the district-wise and religious distribution of the women vendors is given. The following pictures emerge from the table:

A. The market under study, the Khwairamband/the Sana Keithel, is in the Imphal West District. Naturally the sheer logic of locational advantage explains the very dominating proportion of women from this district (75 per cent of the total). The next highest proportion is from the neighbouring district of Imphal East at about 23 per cent of the total.

B. One interesting locational feature of the women vendors is the presence (though naturally small in proportion) of women even from the far-off districts of Thoubal and Bishnupur (25 kms. from the market).[14] This speaks of the spatial coverage of the market and participatory acumen of the women of Manipur. In other words, the economic, social and cultural impact of the market are directly felt, through the women participants, without time gap in areas at least as far as 25 kilometres away from the market centre. This is in addition to the much wider indirect impacts any market would have.

C. When it comes to the religious composition of the women, the composition of the valley population in general gets reflected very well. The proportion Hinduism and Sanamahi followers, both practised by Meitei only, constitute almost 98 per cent of the total. The rest, Islam followers, are Meitei Pangals (Meitei Muslims). They are mostly egg sellers.

Table 3.6: Distribution of Vendors by District [15] and Religion

Name of the district	*Number*	*Religion*			
		Hinduism	*Christianity*	*Islam*	*Sanamahi**
Imphal West	225 (75%)	212 (70.67%)	-	-	13 (4.33%)
Imphal East	68 (22.64%)	55 (18.32%)	-	5 (1.67%)	8 (2.67%)
Bishnupur	3 (1%)	2 (0.67%)	-	-	1 (0.33%)
Thoubal	4 (1.33%)	2 (0.67%)	-	-	2 (0.67%)
Total	300	271 (90.33%)	-	5 (1.67%)	24 (8.00%)

Source: Personal Survey

Note: *Sanamahi - a traditional Meitei religion.

Income Earned Per Day

Income, being the basis of both production and consumption, is an important variable to be examined in every socio-economic context. We have classified the daily income[16] of the vendors into six categories starting from Rs. 300 or less to Rs. 1501 and more, maintaining a range of Rs. 300.[17] Whereas any classification of income categories would have some elements of arbitrariness, the rationale for the adoption of Rs. 300 lies in the possibility of maintaining a family with the profits derived from a sale of Rs. 300. The percentage distribution of the six income categories is shown in Table 3.7.

Table 3.7: Distribution of Women Vendors by Income per day

Category	*Income (Rs.)*	*Number*	*Percentage Distribution*
I	Up to 300	55	18.34
II	301-600	63	21.00
III	601-900	34	11.33
IV	901-1200	68	22.67
V	1201-1500	49	16.33
VI	1501 and above	31	10.33
	Total	300	100

Source: Personal Survey

The following pictures become salient from Table 3.6.

A. Assuming that the relevant families survive mainly on the earnings of the women vendors and also that those enjoying a sale of Rs. 600 or less per day constitute the families living on the margin or near the margin, these constitute as high as 39.34 per cent of the total vendors.

B. In the total category, Rs. 900 turns out to be the dividing line for the half way mark. Those earning Rs. 900 or less constitute about 51 per cent of the total with the rest being those earning higher than Rs. 900.

C. Another interesting feature, or rather just a statistical coincidence, emerging from the table is the decline by about 6 percentage points in the relative proportion of each higher income category above Rs. 900.

D. Individual category-wise, the categories of Rs. 301 – 600 and

Rs. 901 – 1200 each constitute the largest proportions of the total.

E. The overall picture emerging from the table is that the per day sales of each vendor is not high by modern business standards. The proportion of the category of having sales of above Rs. 1500 is low at only 10.33 per cent of the total.

Figure 3.3 represents the percentage distribution of women vendors by their income per day.

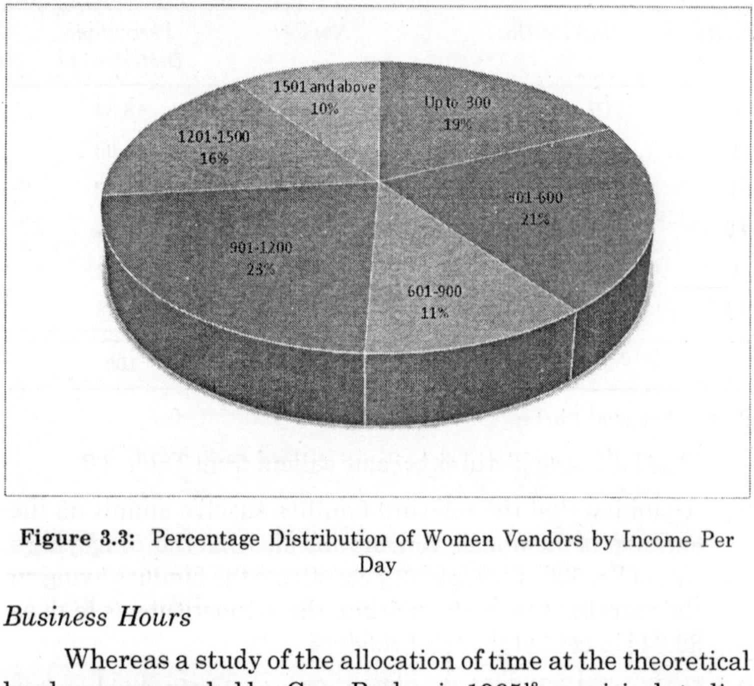

Figure 3.3: Percentage Distribution of Women Vendors by Income Per Day

Business Hours

Whereas a study of the allocation of time at the theoretical level was expounded by Gary Becker in 1965[18], empirical studies of both per se and inter-gender differences in time allocation have now become active areas of research. In this new context, particularly the relative time allocation of women has thrown up many interesting facts and issues for further research.[19] First, there is what Hochschild[20] termed the "*stalled revolution*" wherein increase in participation in the labour market has not been accompanied by a reduction of obligations in the domestic realms of women. This is so particularly because women naturally have the burden of bearing children in addition to participation in the labour market.[21] Secondly, an active literature has emerged examining the determinants of time use and the gender differentials of it.[22] Further academic divide in this connection between sociologists and neo-classical economists is becoming very sharp. While sociologists highlight the role of social institutions in defining the gender division of activities, the economists with the neo-classical bent of mind would explain the gender differentials in occupational activities in terms of incentives, constraints and comparative advantage.[23]

The present research does not, however, have the canvass and the intention of examining gender differentials in time allocation. It has a limited purpose of studying the time women vendors spend in the market, relate it with their income from the participation in the market, and ultimately examine the correlates of these with the status and position of women. This would enable us to categorise the women according to whether their participation is for real returns, for lack of alternatives, for the sake of it, for social networking, or is it a case of plain long hours of work but no alternative.[24] In the light of the above background, we group the women vendors' business hours into five categories. We find cases of women spending 5 hours or a little less than 5 hours in the market and we have taken this as the first category of women according to time classification. At the extreme there are cases of women spending 8 hours or more in the market and we have put this at the highest category. In between these two extremes,we

Table 3.8: Business Hours Distribution of Women Vendors

Category	*Business Hours*	*Number*	*Percentage*
I	<5 hours	4	1.33
II	6 hours	25	8.33
III	7 hours	38	12.67
IV	8 hours	113	37.67
V	>8 hours	120	40.00
	Total	300	100

Source: Personal Survey

have given a classification of 1 hour apart. Table 3.8 is the picture of the percentage distribution of the vendors by business hours.

Table 3.8 reveals the following picture:

A. One major picture emerging from the table is the high proportion of women working 8 hours or more in the market constituting about 80 per cent of the total. Assuming that the global scenario of non-reduction in household responsibilities of women despite their participation in the labour market[25] prevails in Manipur as well, this implies huge work responsibilities and long working hours for the women in this market, with all the potential consequences on health, hygiene and personal leisure.

B. The scenario given in A above gets accentuated if we include the proportion of women spending 7 hours in the higher category. In fact, this proportion of women is as high as about 13 per cent of the total, thereby taking the proportion of women working 7 hours or more in the market to more than 90 per cent of the total. In other words, since these women are present in the market for seven days in a week, more than 90 per cent of the women spend more than 49 hours in a week in the market, and about 80 per cent of the total do so for more than 56 hours in a week.

C. In still other words, three-fourth of the vendors allocate on an average of slightly about 33.33 per cent of the total number of hours available in a week to the market. This is much higher than the average working hours per week seen elsewhere.[26]

D. The proportion of women spending five hours or less per day in the market, though existent, is very small constituting only a little over 1 per cent of the total.

E. The proportion of vendors who followed 6 hours as their business timings is 8.33 per cent of the total.

The overall implication emerging from Table 3.8 is the active participation, as measured by devotion of time to market, of women in the market activities as exemplified by the positive relationship between proportion of women and the number of hours spent in the market. This naturally leads to the usual economic question of enquiring into the incentives or other driving forces behind this revealed behaviour.[27]

Figure 3.4 shows the percentage distribution of women vendors by business hours.

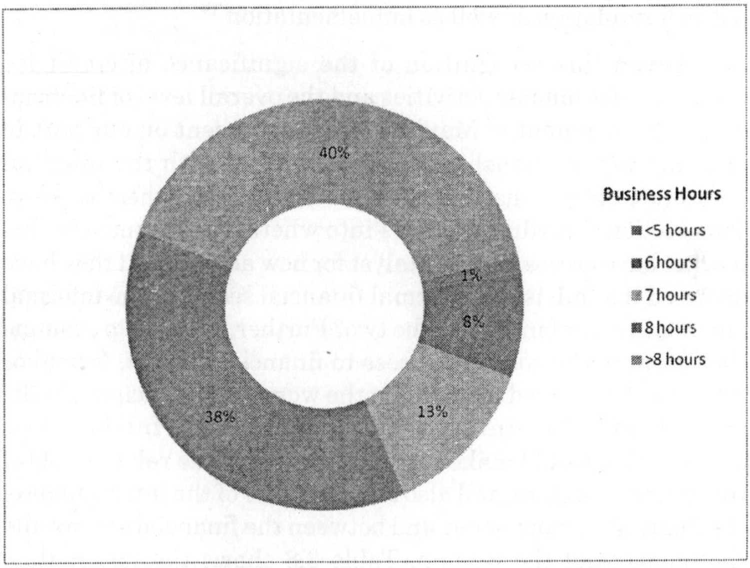

Figure 3.4: Percentage Distribution of Women Vendors by Business Hours

Women Vendors, Financial Institutions and Non-Institutional Creditors

Every economy necessitates the emergence of new and newer economic activities for its sustained growth. Here the importance of credit for starting new economic activities has been recognised by economists since Schumpeter highlighted its significance in the beginning of the twentieth century.[28] In addition to the corporate sectors' requirements, the need for credit intervention is now being emphasized with renewed vigour for generation of self-employment activities and general removal of poverty.

It is in this context that the crucial role of credit providing financial intermediaries arises. While earlier the traditional financial institutions, like village moneylenders, were playing this role, their exploitative and the deterrent-to-productivity nature has been extensively recorded in the literature. This is why the spread and depth of modern financial institutions governed by government regulations are given high priority in development policy formulation as well as implementation.[29]

Given this recognition of the significance of credit for initiation of economic activities and the overall level of financial sector development of Manipur, it is incumbent on our part to examine the relationship the vendors have with the financial institutions, traditional or modern, in the conduct of their business. This section accordingly delves into whether the women in this market have access to this catalyst for new activities. If they have accessed it at all, is it the formal financial sector or the informal one or still a combination of the two? Further, we need to examine the extent of the role this access to financial market, formal or informal, has played in enabling the women to participate in the market and sustaining their business. Still further, this examination would make it possible to study the relative role of the financial sectors, and also the dynamics of the interactions of the financial sectors per se and between the financial sectors and the business of the women. Table 3.8 shows the information relating to source of financial assistance taken and the proportion of the vendors which have taken assistance.

Before we interpret the Table 3.9, it would be in place to explain the terms Micro-finance Institutions and Non- Institutional Creditors as implied by the women. The Micro-finance Institutions, which the women in this market have accessed, are private sector players. They have come to play a role in the women's market in order to exploit the situation arising out of two conditions. First, naturally the women in this market need credit on a small scale but definitely on daily or weekly bases. Secondly, the public sector or formal sector banks are conspicuous by their absence in interventions in this atmosphere. So, these private sector agencies have come into the fray to fill this void. But they are not much different from the traditional moneylenders except that they have an air of formality in their organisation and management.

Table 3.9: Percentage Distribution of Vendors According to Financial Assistance from Micro-Finance Institutions or Non-Institutional Creditors

Financial Assistance taken or not									
Yes									
Micro-Finance Institutions		*Non-Institutional Creditors*		*Micro-Finance Institutions and Non-Institutional Creditors*		*Total*		*No*	
Number	*Percentage*	*Number*	*Percentage*	*Number*	*Percentage*	*Number*	*Percentage*	*Number*	*Percentage*
107	35.7	43	14.3	55	18.3	205	68.3	95	31.7

Source: Personal Survey

The Non-Institutional Creditors as the very name implies are the traditional moneylenders. Unlike others, they are individuals who thrive on charging interest at rates exorbitant by any standards. The one convenience this source has over the formal modern banks is the absence of processing time, and consequently the quickness of disbursal of loans. Besides, these moneylenders do not ask for the mortgaging of vendors licences with them unlike the private micro-finance institutions.

Given the above description of sources of finance of the women vendors, we can now proceed to interpreting Table 3.9.

A. The most prominent picture emerging from the survey of source of finance of the women vendors is the absolute absence of the public sector banks in a context where all the banks were nationalised in 1969 and private sector banks are still a far cry in this part of the country. This speaks of both relative and absolutely higher interest burden the women are bearing, given the interest charges pattern explained above.

B. More than two-thirds (68.3 per cent) of the women have taken loans from the sources explained above. The private sector organised moneylenders have now emerged as the most significant player. About 36 per cent of the total (or 52 per cent of those who have taken loans) have taken loans from these organisations. This relatively higher presence of the group as moneylenders is the lower rate of interest charged by them as compare to the other group of individual moneylenders. We must, however, hasten to add that they charge interest at the rate much higher than that of the public sector banks.

C. The private moneylenders are still a major player in the credit market here with more than 14 per cent of the total (or 21 per cent of those who have taken loans) vendors having borrowed from them.

D. In the case of about 18 per cent of the total (or about 27 per cent of those who have taken loans), there is incidence of having taking loans from both the sources.

Table 3.10: Distribution of Non-loanee Vendors by their Nature of Work

Sl. No.	*Nature of work*	*Number of Vendors*	*Number of Non-loanee Vendors*	*Column IV as Percentage of Column III*	*Nature of Effects*
I	*II*	*III*	*IV*	*V*	*VI*
1	Fruit Vendor	32	12	37.5	Scale effect
2	Vegetable Vendor	43	11	25.58	Scale effect
3	Fish Vendor	52	10	19.23	Product differentiation
4	Clothes Vendor	108	24	22.22	Product differentiation
5	Pots Vendor	3	2	66.67	Scale effect
6	Rice Vendor	6	3	50	Scale effect
7	Knife Vendor	5	3	60	Scale effect
8	Quilts Vendor	7	4	57.14	Scale effect
9	Eggs Vendor	5	4	80	Scale effect
10	Betel Leaf Vendor	5	3	60	Scale effect
11	Local lamp Vendor	2	2	100	Scale effect
12	Mat Vendor	5	1	33.33	Scale effect
13	Jewellery Vendor	6	3	50	Scale effect
14	Dry Channa Vendor	5	3	60	Scale effect
15	Eateries	8	5	62.5	Scale effect
16	Utensils for rituals Vendor	3	2	66.67	Scale effect
17	Mattress Vendor	5	2	40	Scale effect
18	Doll Vendor	2	1	50	Scale effect
19	*Total*	*300*	*95*	-	-

Source: Personal Survey
Computed from Table 3.9

Here a special explanation of the 32 per cent (31.67 per cent to be exact) of the vendors, who have not availed of any loan facility from any credit extending agency, is called for. Since this proportion is high and also since 68 per cent others have taken loans, it naturally invites the question as to why they have not followed suit. The number of non-loanee vendors with their nature of work is shown in Table 3.10. But to have a better understanding and appreciation of Table 3.10, we need to be clear on some points.

As understandable, the women vendors do business in different groups of product items. It needs to mention at this point that there is product differentiation in some groups namely fishes and clothes vendors. This product differentiation further impacts upon the level of working capital requirements for each differentiated product. For instance, among the fish vendors, there are vendors who vend fresh fishes and others dried fishes. Within both fresh and dry fishes, there is product differentiation again in terms of larger and smaller species. Those who do business in the larger species, whether fresh or dried, naturally require higher working capital, while in general business in fresh fishes demands a higher working capital. In the case of remaining groups of vendors, the effect is rather of scale than of product differentiation. This scale effect gets reflected naturally in the volume of working capital requirements of the vendors.

The predominance of scale effect in majority of the groups of vendors naturally has implications on whether a vendor goes for loan or otherwise.

Given the above background, we can now proceed to interpret Table 3.10 and Table 3.11.

From Table 3.10, the following pictures emerge:

A. It comes out clearly from Table 3.10 that the proportion of non-loanees is lowest in the two groups of business, fish and clothes, where product differentiation is the norm rather than predominance of scale effects. In other words, majority of the vendors in these two lines of business have taken loans.

B. As a corollary of the first implication, we find that in 12 out of the 16 groups of vendors where scale effect dominates 50 to 100 per cent of the vendors are non-loanees. Of these pots (66.67 per cent), eggs (80 per cent), local lamp (100 per cent), betel leaf (60 per cent), dry channa (60 per cent), utensils for rituals (66.67

per cent) and eateries (62.5 per cent) are businesses of relatively lower working capital requirements.

Table 3.11 endeavours to provide (a) picture of the non-loanees by their Per Day Income categories, and (b) the relative dispersion of the non-loanees (and ipso facto of the loanees). The following major pictures emerge from Table 3.11.

I. When we examine the proportion of non-loanees in the total number of vendors, the predominance of loanees is established in all income categories except in Rs. 601-900. The relative shares of non-loanees are far lower than the relative shares of income categories in the total number of vendors surveyed, thereby implying majority of the vendors having been resorted to borrowing from one source or the other.

II. Of the total number of non-loanees, almost 84 per cent belong to the first three income categories. Since this group belongs to the lower income categories, we may venture to hypobooke at this stage on the possible reasons for their behaviour. First, it could be that their scale of business does not call for additional financing. Second, since their scale of business is small the creditors might not be finding them attractive. Third, it could as well be plain hesitation on the part of the vendors to borrow as they might be worried about repayment options.

III. Of the total number of non-loanees (95), 37 (about 39 per cent) have received financial assistance from the family. In this group also the predominance of the first three categories in the total is salient in accounting for 89 per cent of the total of 37. This throws up another more plausible explanation of why the vendors, particularly in the first three categories up to Rs 601-900, have not gone for borrowing. It is likely that the vendors who have neither received assistance from family nor borrowed from the moneylenders are working on anxious margins.

Figures 3.5 and 3.6 are diagrammatic representation of the distribution of vendors by loanees and non-loanees. While Figure 3.5 depicts the distribution of non-loanees by income categories, Figure 3.6 shows the distribution of non-loanees by family support and absolute non-loanees.[30]

Table 3.11: Distribution of Non-Loanee Vendors by Their Per Day Income

Income (Rs.)	*Number*	*Number of Non-loanee vendors*	*Column III as Percentage of Column II Total*	*Number of Non-loanee vendors who get financial support from family members*	*Column V as percentage of Column II*	*Column V as percentage of Column II Total*	*Number of Non-loanee vendors who neither take financial support from family members nor from any financial institutions*	*Column VIII as Percentage of Column II*	*Column VIII as Percentage of Column II Total*
I	*II*	*III*	*IV*	*V*	*VI*	*VII*	*VIII*	*IX*	*X*
Up to 300	55 (18.34%)	27 (28.4%)	9	10 (27.03%)	18.18	3.33	17 (29.31%)	30.9	5.67
301-600	63 (21.00%)	21 (22.1%)	7	6 (16.22%)	9.5	2	15 (25.86%)	23.81	5
601-900	34 (11.33%)	32 (33.7%)	10.7	17 (45.94%)	50	5.67	15 (25.86%)	44.12	5
901-1200	68 (22.67%)	5 (5.2%)	1.7	1 (2.7%)	1.47	0.33	4 (6.9%)	5.88	1.33
1201-1500	49 (16.33%)	3 (3.2%)	1	-	-	-	3 (5.17%)	6.12	1
1500 and above	31 (10.33%)	7 (7.4%)	2.3	3 (8.11%)	9.7	1	4 (6.9%)	12.9	1.33
Total	300	*95*	*31.7*	*37*		*11.33*	*58*		*19.33*

Note: The figures within parentheses are the percentages of the column total.

Source: Personal Survey

Computed from Table 3.9

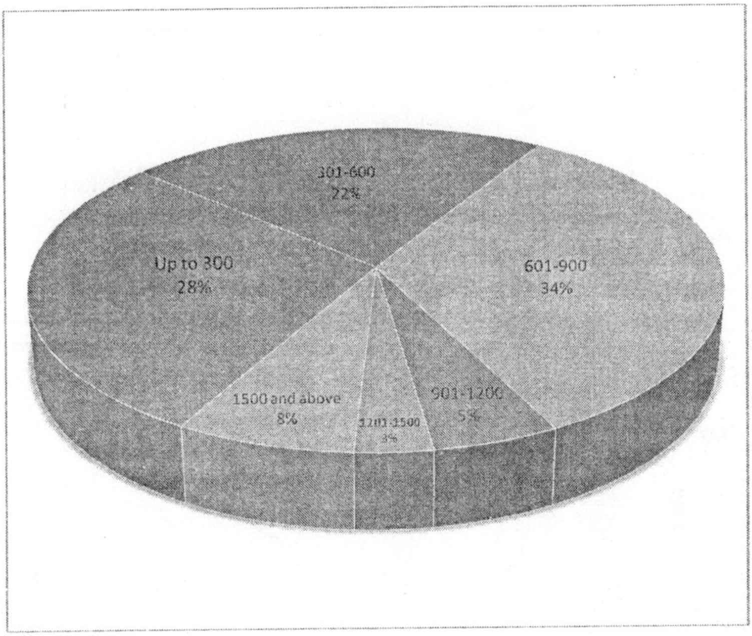

Figure 3.5: Distribution of Non-loanee vendors by their per day income

Financial Assistance from Family Members

We have seen above that there are vendors who have received financial support from family members. As seen above, there are vendors who would not avail loans from outside for various reasons. First, one may not have the kind of knowledge and network to access credit facilities of either the formal or informal financiers. Secondly, one may be plain scared of taking loan for fear of inability to repay. Thirdly, one may not be requiring capital to run business to the extent to necessitate loans from outside sources. Fourth, the terms of financial support from the financiers might be found to be prohibitive. Fifth, one may be having internal resources of support from own family members (close relatives). In this section, accordingly we examine deeper into this category of vendors who have received family support.

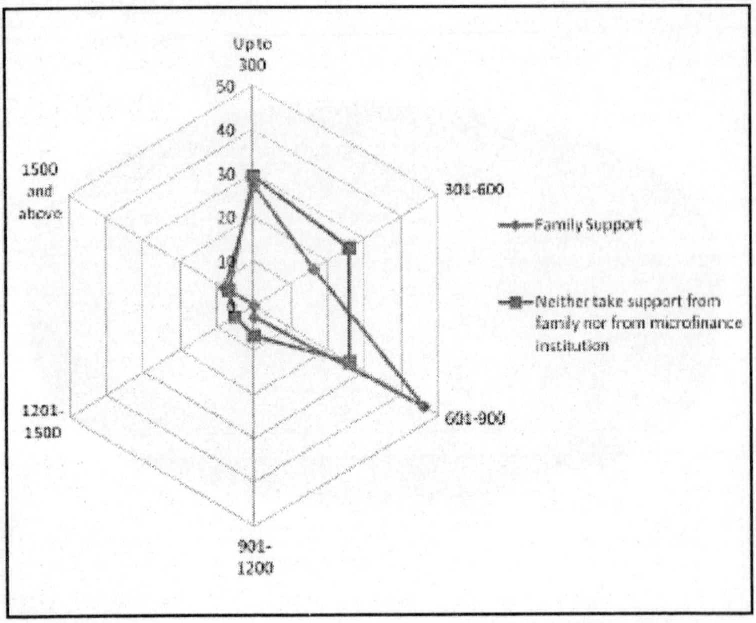

Figure 3.6: Distribution of Non-loanee Vendors by Family Support and Absolute Non-Loanees

Tables 3.12 and 3.13 provide picture of those who have availed financial assistance from the family members.

Table 3.12: Percentage Distribution of Vendors by Financial Assistance from Family

Financial assistance takenfrom their family members or not	*Number*	*Percentage Distribution*
Yes	107	35.67
No	193	64.33

Source: Personal Survey

Table 3.13: Distribution of Vendors who took Financial Assistance from Family by their Per Day Income

Income (Rs.)	*Number*	*Number of Vendors who took Financial Assistance from their Family*	*Column III as Percentage of Column II Column III as Percentage of Column II*	*Total*
I	*II*	*III*	*IV*	*V*
Up to 300	55(18.34%)	32(29.9%)	58.18	10.67
301-600	63(21.00%)	16(14.95%)	25.4	5.33
601-900	34 (11.33%)	29(27.1%)	85.29	9.67
901-1200	68 (22.67%)	14(13.08%)	20.59	4.67
1201-1500	49 (16.33%)	9(8.42%)	18.37	3
1500 and above	31(10.33%)	7(6.54%)	22.58	2.33
Total	300	107		35.67

Note: The figures within parentheses are the percentages of the column total.

The following points emerge from Tables 3.12 and 3.13:

A. The proportion of vendors who took financial assistance from their family members was about 36 per cent of the total. Taking financial assistance from the family has several implications. First, it speaks of the strength of the family ties while at the same time has the potential to strengthen the ties within the family members. Second, it also has the purpose of serving the urgency of the vendors with ease and a sense of togetherness. Thirdly and in the case of those who took loans from financial institutions or moneylenders, the reason could be supplementing each source for larger scale of business. Above all, receiving financial assistance from the family members would, other things remaining the same, involve least transaction costs.

B. A substantial proportion of vendors (64.33 per cent) do not take any financial support from their family members. Whereas the reasons for not taking or receiving any financial assistance from any family member were not specifically inquired into, we may conjecture some possible ones. First, it could be either the vendor herself was the only earner in the family and her earn income was directed toward the support of the family. Second, it could be that the familial milieu was not for asking financial assistance. Third, it could as well be that the financial assistance was not provided though asked for.

C. It is clear from Table 3.13 that taking financial assistance from the family members is a characteristic across all the income categories; the range of this spreads from 18.37 per cent of the Rs. 1201 – 1500 category to 85.29 per cent of the Rs. 601 – 900 category. The reasons for this prevalence naturally would correspond to those given in the above two explanations.

Comparison of Vendors' Income with Income of their Husbands

As stated above passim Manipuri woman plays an important economic role. As being so, it will be more fruitful if we illustrate the vendor's income relative with the income of husband. This will establish the distinctiveness of the women's contribution, besides enabling us to understand the stage of economic empowerment of women in the State. This is exactly what it is being attempted in this section.

Table 3.14 gives us the relative picture of the income of women vendors and their husbands.

Table 3.14: Vendors' Income vis-a-vis Husband's Income

	Number	*Percentage distribution*
More than what the husband earns	117	56.25
Less than what the husband earns	59	28.37
About the same	32	15.38
Total	208	100

Source: Personal Survey

The table 3.14 reveals that about 56 per cent of the vendors earn more than what their husbands do. These vendors were naturally the main income earners of their respective families.[31] The husbands of these women are either non-working or, if working at all, work in the informal sector. If we add to this the more than 15 per cent of vendors who earn more or less equal to their husbands' earnings, the pre-eminence of the women vendors in the economic front is obvious. The proportion of the vendors who reported earning less than that of their husbands, on the other hand, was about 28 per cent of the total. The husbands of these vendors were mostly working in the organised sector like government offices while some were doing business. Here we must hasten to add that the fact of earnings being less than that of husbands does not necessarily imply low earning or an earning relatively less than that of other women vendors but only that their husbands happen to be working in sectors enjoying relatively higher wages and income; there are of course low income cases though.

Distance Travelled and Mode of Transport

Distance travelled between home and market is an important determinant of time and monetary cost of transport, which has naturally implications for the profit margin. It is also an important determinant of the time a vendor can spend in the market; closer to the market one can afford to be there for longer hours. Proximity is the important variable here. It is in this light that we have gathered information on the distance a vendor travels and the mode of transport she utilises.

As was seen, majority of the vendors (98% - 75% from Imphal West and 23% from Imphal East) are from the vicinity of the market. In other words, it is found that 98 per cent of the vendors are from within five kilometres of the market. This implies that there is not much difference in time costs of travel among the vendors.

The different means of transport adopted by the vendors to reach the market are by foot, cycle-rickshaw, auto-rickshaw, jeep and bus. The cycle-rickshaw turns out to be the most widely used means of transport accounting for almost 55 per cent of the vendors,

Table 3.15: Percentage Distribution of Vendors by their Mode of Transport

Mode of Transport	*Number*	*Percentage Distribution*
By foot	20	6.67
Cycle Rickshaw	165	55.00
Jeep	65	21.67
Auto-Rickshaw	43	14.33
Bus	7	2.33
Total	300	100

followed by jeep (21.67 per cent), auto-rickshaw (14.33 per cent), walking (6.67 per cent) and bus (2.33 per cent) in that order. If we look at it in another way, 61.67 per cent of the vendors use non-motorised transport of foot and cycle-rickshaw whereas the remaining 38.33 per cent use motorised transport of jeep[32], auto-rickshaw and bus. This implies that 93 per cent of the vendors spend some amount each day for commuting to the market. The proportion of vendors by their mode of transport and fare from home to market (back and forth) is shown in Table 3.15 and 3.16 respectively.

Table 3.16: Percentage Distribution of Vendors by Fare from Home to Market (Back and Forth)

Fare	*Number*	*Percentage Distribution*
<Rs.10	27	9.64
Rs.10-Rs.15	187	66.79
Rs.15-Rs.20	46	16.43
>Rs.20	20	7.14
Total	280	100

Business Experience of Women Vendors' in another Market before the Present One

Table 3.16 depicts the women vendors who started their business activity in another market before shifting to this present Khwairamband Keithel.

Table 3.16: Percentage Distribution of Women's Vendors by Business Experience in another Market before the Present One

Business Experience before the Present one	*Number*	*Percentage*
Yes	5	1.67
No	295	98.33
Total	300	100
Place of the Former Market	Number	Percentage
In the same district	3	60
In the another district	2	40
Total	5	100
Reasons for leaving the Earlier Market	Number	Percentage
Shifting of home	-	-
Less Profit	5	100
Fewer Customer	-	-
Conflict with neighbouring vendor	-	-
Others	-	-
Total	5	100

Source: Personal Survey.

From the Table 3.16, it is evident that only a marginal proportion, i.e. only 1.67 per cent of the total vendors is found to have shifted to this marketing place from other market. Among these vendors (5), 60 per cent (3) from the same district of Imphal West while 40 per cent (2) were from other districts. The only reason for leaving the earlier market cited by the vendors is higher profit in the current market. This is understandable because the

Sana-Keithel/Khwairamband Keithel is the dominant market place in the State.

Conclusion

In the previous two chapters we have emphasized the necessity of examining the role and status of Manipuri women in the light of the global trend in both theory and empirics. The Sanakeithel of Manipur has been one most enduring institution reflecting these issues in relation to the women of the State. An appreciation of the position of women in this market would invariably enable us to understand the dynamics of women's status. This is done on the basis of responses to a structured questionnaire. While this has been a cross-sectional survey, the results gain much significance when situated in the light of data of different historical epochs. Three important pictures emerge from such an endeavour. First, the participation of women in outside-the-household activities continues to be still robust. Secondly, this participation cuts across the levels of academic qualification the women might possess. Thirdly, the institutional mechanism of this participation has always moved ahead of the times in the sense that the absence of supporting traditional or modern financial institutions has not deterred the continuation or expansion.

NOTES & REFERENCES

1. Kate, A., and Niels, G. (2008), "The Relevant Market: A Concept Still in Search of A Definition", *Journal of Competition Law and Economics*, Oxford University Press, London, pp.1-37.

2. Khemani, R.S. and Shapiro, D.M. (1993), *Glossary of Industrial Organisation Economics and Competition Law*, commissioned by the Directorate for Financial, Fiscal and Enterprise Affairs, OECD.

3. Saxena, H.M. (1988), *Rural Markets and Development*, Chapter II, Rawat Publications, Jaipur, pp.11-12.

4. Mulvihill, D.F., and Mulvihill, R.L. (1970), *Geography, Marketing and Urban Growth*, Van Nostrand, p.9.

5. Hodder, B.W., and Lee, R. (1974), *Economic Geography*, Metheun, London, p.137.

6. See, Pirenne, H., (1936), *Economic and Social History of Medieval Europe*, New York; Polanyi, K., (1957), *Trade and Markets in Early Empires*, Glencoe; and Berry, B.L.J., (1967), *Geography of Market Centres and Retail Distribution*, Printice-Hall.

7. See, for instance, Besley, Timothy (2007), "The New Political Economy", *The Economic Journal*, pp. 570-587.
8. Kotler, P. and Zaltman, G. (1971), "Social Marketing: An Approach to Planned Social Change", *Journal of Marketing,* Chicago, Vol.35, p. 5. For details one may refer Cleef (1937, reprinted 1971), Berry (1967), Peter Scott (1970), R.L. Davies (1976), Garnier and Delobez (1979), Wanmali (1981) and Saxena (1984).
9. Jain, D., and Asem, S., (2007), "A Feminist Mart – Women's Empowerment", *Deccan Herald,* 26th October 2007.
10. Details of the market and the survey have been given in Chapter 1.
11. There are instances like a vegetable vendor enjoying a meal from a food vendor in exchange for some vegetable items. These we may not call barter in the strict traditional sense for the food as well as the vegetables have explicit monetized values. Such transactions constitute only about one per cent of the total transactions in the market.
12. A copy of the Questionnaire used in the Survey is attached as Appendix I.
13. In the literature a joint family is usually considered to be a traditional one whereas a nuclear family a modern one. The more or less equally high proportion of women from both of these implies the participation of women in the labourforce irrespective of the family type. This corroborates the widely held belief of social tolerance of women's participation in activities outside the household.
14. The low percentage of vendors in these districts was in the population itself and not due to distribution in the sample.
15. Manipur has nine districts. The four valley districts are Imphal East, Imphal West, Thoubal and Bishnupur districts, and the five mountain districts are Senapati, Tamenglong, Churachandpur, Chandel and Ukhrul.
16. Here the concept of income equals the daily sales value of each vendor. So we are using the terms sales and income interchangeably.
17. While classifying into income categories we are not yet taking into consideration the differences in the nature of engagement of the vendors.
18. Becker, G., (1965), "A Theory of Allocation of Time," *Economic Journal,* Vol. 75, pp. 493-517.

19. See for instance, Ilahi, N., (2001), "Gender and the Allocation of Adult Time: Evidence from the Peru LSMS Panel Data", The World Bank, *Working Paper No. 2744*; Medeiros, M., Guerreiro, R., Osorio, Costa, J., (2007), "Gender Inequalities in Allocating Time to Paid and Unpaid Work: Evidence from Bolivia, International Poverty Centre", *Working Paper No. 34*; and Anxo, D., Flood, L., Mencarine, L., Pailhe, A., Solez, A., Letizia, M. Tanturri, (2007), "Time Allocation between Work and Family over the Life-Cycle: A Comparative Gender Analysis of Italy, France, Sweden and the United States", *IZA Discussion Paper No. 3193*, November and the references cited in these papers.

20. Hochschild, A., (1989), *The Second Shift: Working Parents and the Revolution at Home*, Viking, New York.

21. This is what we call dual burden in literature.

22. See, for example, King, E., and Evenson, E. Robert, (1983), "Time Allocation and Home Production in Phillipine Rural Households", in Buvinic, M., Lycette, M. A and McGreevey, W. P, eds, *Women and Poverty in the Third World*, Johns Hopkins University Press, Baltimore; Khandker, Shahidur, R., (1988), "Determinants of Women's Time Allocation in Rural Bangladesh", *Economic Development and Cultural Change*, Vol.37, pp. 111-126; Alderman, Harold and Chisti, S., (1991), "Simultaneous Determination of Household and Market-Oriented Activities of Women in Rural Pakistan," *Research in Population Economics*, Vol. 7, pp.245-265; and Fafchamps, Marcel and Agnes, R. Quisimbing, (1998), *Social Roles, Human Capital and the Intra household Division of Labour: Evidence from Pakistan*, Department of Economics, Stanford University, Mimeograph.

23. This approach is the one pioneered by Becker (1965).

24. Cf. Bandasi, E. and Wodon, Q.,(2009), Working Long Hours and Having No Choice: Time Poverty in Guinea, Gender Group, Poverty Reduction and Economic Management Network, Human Development Network, Development Dialogue on Values and Ethics, World Bank, *Working Paper No. 4961,* June.

25. In this regard, see, for instance, the work of Hochschild, A., (1989).

26. In Pakistan, for instance, the working hours for women in the informal sector is found to be 37 hours per week, while 40 hours for the formal sector. See Nazli, H., (2007), "Rural Women and Empowerment: An Economic Perspective from Pakistan", in Arunachalam, J., and U. Kalpagam, (2007), ed., *op.cit.*, p.102.

27. These and other related issues are taken up for enquiry in Chapter 4.

28. Schumpeter, J., (1961), *The Theory of Economic Development: An Inquiry into Profits, Capital, Credit, Interest and the Business Cycle*, Oxford University Press, New York. As he said, "[One] can only become an entrepreneur by previously becoming a debtor." p. 102.

29. The vast literature on Schumpeterian economics and the various Plan programmes of the Government of India, e.g., are testimony to this.

30. By absolute non-loanees, we mean those who have neither taken loans from any lender nor received financial assistance from family.

31. The same case is also found in the 1996 Latvian Household Budget Survey where an estimated 44 percent of Latvian children live in households where women are the main earners and the economic welfare of a large number of children depends directly on the employment prospects of their mothers. Referred by Malhotra, *op.cit.*, p. 165.

32 Jeeps are recent but very popular taxi service.

4

Participation and Empowerment

Introduction

In the foregoing two chapters, we have attempted to provide a picture of the role and position of Manipuri women right from pre-colonial period to the present times. This has been supplemented by a contemporary profile of vendors in Khwairamband Keithel (Women's Market) based on personal structured survey. The distinctive role women have been playing in the socio-politico-economic realm of life was evident. The active participation of women in all the three sectors of the economy and particularly in activities conducted outside the households was also salient. This speaks of the freedom with which women in Manipur enjoyed for participation in activities outside the household. While a definitive statement on the level of freedom women enjoyed inside the household cannot be made at this juncture, the active participation in activities outside the household prompts one to assume the prevalence of relatively satisfactory level of freedom inside the household.

If we couple this with the historically acclaimed political uprisings of women (the *Nupilals*), a staunch feminist would term the period a "Women's World".[1] In any case, we can safely vouch that there has been in existence in Manipur at least a rather more than less equality between the sexes. This sense of equality springs from the prime role women play in enhancing household production as well as bringing an additional income to the family. It is as if time has not changed this.

Women of Manipur still retain their character and role. A living testimony is the women's market in Khwairamband Keithel. The players in the market are still preserving and maintaining the peculiar elements and ideologies which identify their own culture and traditions relating to the historical role of women. As argued in Chapter 2, the institution of *Lallup Kaba* might have been one catalytic push factor for women to increasingly participate in activities outside the household. Another factor might be geographic[2] whereby the women of Manipur are more oriented towards work rather than idling around as routine housewives. This context establishes the important economic role of women in household maintenance within the broad social view of men as breadwinners.

In this background, it is now incumbent on our part to examine three issues. First, at this juncture of history, we need to study as to whether the inherent traits of women as mentioned above are still prevalent or otherwise. Secondly, we should now be exploring as to whether the traditional push and pull factors influencing the participation of women in economic activities outside the household are still effective and/or reinforced. Third, we should also be delving into whether new push and pull factors are in emergence or not. In this chapter, we attempt to address these three issues by studying vendor-women in the Khwairamband Keithel.

Here in passing it would be relevant to recall briefly the international and the national perspectives regarding the participation of women in the labour market. In a study, the ILO[3]identifies two reasons for this: (a) Women's economic need, and (b) national necessity for increased production.[4]Coming to India, the Ministry of Labour[5] has opined that, irrespective of the stage of economic or social development of a country, four factors prevail which lead women to join the working force. They are: (a) the inadequate income of the principal earner of the family; (b) mishaps, such as incapacity or incapacitation of the family breadwinner; (c) death of the breadwinner; and (d) a woman's desire for economic independence and higher standard of living. Some other studies have also brought to light the fact that loneliness is also a motive behind women seeking employment outside their homes.[6]

Why Women Work?: A Case of Khwairamband Keithel

We have now understood the international as well as national perspective on why women come to join the labour market. We have also emphasized the issues of women work participation outside their home in the context of Manipur. In what follows, we shall be endeavouring to examine these issues by looking closely into the responses of the women in the Khwairamband Keithel; Khwairamband Keithel is arguably the most important labour market institutions for women in Manipur.

Main Reasons for Labour Market Participation

For the convenience of analysis, we have classified the reasons for women joining the work force in the Khwairamband Keithel into two main categories as follows:

1. Financial reasons; and
2. Non-financial reasons.

1. Financial Reasons: The financial reasons comprise of three sub-reasons, viz., (a) Economic pressures, (b) Other economic needs, and (c) Higher standard of living. Economic pressures are those pertaining to the fulfilment of basic minimum needs of life of the family and self. Other economic needs, on the other hand, are those involving intentions to help relatives and to meet the medical and health expenses of self. The third reason of higher standard of living concerns the universal phenomenon of longing for better living.

2. Non-financial Reasons: The non-financial reason consists of (a) Personality traits, (b) To utilize time, and (c) Traditional occupation. Personality traits represent the desire of women vendors to prove themselves socially and economically. It also includes working for personal independence and insurance against future uncertainties. The second category of utilising time reflects the efforts of vendors to escape from their daily drudgery and instead devote the time to meaningful calls. Certain families have been engaged in this occupation for generations. This is being sustained by the present generation as well. We have termed this as traditional reasons.

In Table 4.1 we give a picture of the reasons driving the women for participation in the labour market and as given by the women themselves.

The major points emerging from Table 4.1 are as follows:

A. By and large the scenario emerging from the table is the overriding predominance of financial reasons as the compelling force for women to join the labour market in the Khwairamband Keithel. As is evident from the table, as high as 85 per cent of the women have joined this labour market on financial considerations alone.

B. A more revealing picture emerges from the table if we look into the detailed classification of the two main reasons.[7] Here, two sub-reasons under Economic Pressure of the financial reasons, viz., meeting basic minimum needs and to fill the gap arising out of the death of the male breadwinner of the family, are of special prominence. These two closely related reasons account for about 71 per cent of the vendors joining the labour force. If we add the rise in the cost of living to these two reasons, together they account for 76 per cent of the total.[8]

C. Another important driving force is the desire of women to spend time effectively. About 12 per cent of the women are in this labour market to utilise the time available to them.

Labour Market Participation by Socio-Demographic Variables

The financial reasons, thus, seem to be the most important reasons for women's seeking employment.[9] However, it is possible that reasons for labour market participation display variations by socio-demographic variables. In what follows we endeavour to examine such variations by age, type of family, education, size of family, marital status and number of earners.

Age

Ceteris paribus, one should expect, within the framework of financial reasons being the predominant reason, that the financial requirement should be more intense and widespread among the younger groups of the vendors. This is because the need for establishing the family and child upbringing requirements should be more among this group than among the more aged ones. Instances for more financial reasons among the latter should most

Table 4.1: Main Reasons for Labour Market Participation

Main Reasons for Work	*Subsidiary Reasons*		*Number*	*Percent*
Non-Financial Reasons	i) Personality Traits	a) Social Recognition	3	1.00
		b) Personal Independence	4	1.33
		Sub-Total	7	2.33
	ii) To Utilize Time	c) To Utilize Time	35	11.67
	iii) Traditional Occupation	d) Traditional Occupation	3	1.00
		Sub-Total	45	15.00
Financial Reasons	i) Economic Pressure	a) Basic minimum needs	136	45.33
		b) Death of the male breadwinner	76	25.33
		c) Rise in the cost of living	15	5.00
		d) Repayment of family debts	4	1.33
		Sub-Total	231	77
	ii) Other Economic Needs	a) To support relatives	9	3.00
		b) To meet health and medical expenses	5	1.67
		Sub-Total	14	4.67
	iii) Higher Standard of Living	a) Education of children and to live decently	10	3.33
		Sub-total	255	85.00
	Total		300	100

Table 4.2: Main Reasons for Employment by Age

Age Group	Financial reasons								Non-financial reasons							
	Economic pressures		Other Economic needs		Higher standard of living		Total	Column VIII as the % of total number of vendors	Personality traits		To utilize time		Traditional occupation		Total	Column xvi the number of vendors
	Number	Percent	Number	Percent	Number	Percent			Number	Percent	Number	Percent	Number	Percent		
I	II	III	IV	V	VI	VII	VIII	IX	X	XI	XII	XIII	XIV	XV	XVI	XVII
25-34	3	50	1	16.67	2	33.33	6 (100%)	2.00	0	0	0	0	0	0	0	0
35-44	25	58.14	3	6.98	2	4.65	30 (69.77%)	10.00	4	9.3	8	18.61	1	2.32	13 (30.23%)	4.33
45-54	62	71.26	6	6.88	4	4.59	72 (82.73%)	24.00	1	1.14	16	18.39	–	–	17 (17.27%)	5.67
55-64	85	89.47	2	2.11	2	2.11	89 (93.69%)	29.67	–	–	6	6.31	–	–	6 (6.31%)	2.00
65-74	50	89.5	–	–	–	–	50 (89.5%)	16.67	1	1.75	2	3.5	2	3.5	5 (10.5%)	1.67
75-84	6	60	–	–	–	–	6 (60%)	2.00	1	10	2	20	1	10	4 (40%)	1.33
85+	1	50	–	–	–	–	1 (50%)	0.33	–	–	1	50	–	–	1 (50%)	0.33

Source: Personal Survey

Note: The figures within parentheses are the percentages of the relevant row total.

probably be for unfortunate[10] reasons befalling the family. Age profile distribution by different reasons is shown in Table 4.2.

The age group distribution of women in this table follows the one adopted earlier in the book. This table gives a picture of the distribution of forces driving the women to participate in the market in each age group category as well as comparative picture of it across different categories. There are two ways for looking for in the table. First, we should be examining the intra-age group distribution of the factors for participation. Secondly, we should as well be examining the inter-age group distribution of the factors for participation. While doing so, the following main pictures emerge from the table:

1. As was established earlier, pure economic reasons constitute the most important driving force for the participation of women in the market. The intra-age group proportion of this ranges from 50 per cent of the age groups of 25-34 and 85+ to 89.5 of the 55-64 and 65–74 age groups.
2. The proportion of women participating in the market for pure economic needs get higher in the older age group categories. In fact, pure economic compulsions constitute the most important driving force for almost 90 per cent of the women between the ages of 55 and 74. The implication of this can be many. One, it can imply that the overall scenario of the economy is not conducive to the wellbeing of the population such that even the aged women are forced to come out to the market to assist the family in the battle for livelihood. Two, it can also imply that in the form of allowing the women to participate in the economic activities, we are somehow exploiting the women force of the State. Three, if we are to attach a longitudinal interpretation to this cross-section data, the implication could be that the women find themselves in a circle of continual confinement to the initial conditions of livelihood without a perceptive rise in wellbeing.
3. The second result gets reinforced by the picture emerging from the responses being given to the intention to help relatives. When young and joins the market first, one starts with the youthful ideal of helping others with the possible returns from

the participation. But this ideal gets fast dissipated as the age advances in to the next higher category, and almost disappears as one reaches the age of 65. This implies that the capability of anyone helping others with the returns from participation does not improve with age and years of participation, but rather gets bogged down by the daily struggles for livelihood. Further, if we take the percentage of about seven in the age categories of 35 – 44 and 45 – 54 as the actual proportions willing and able to help others as this proportion is the only stable one characterizing two different age groups spanning a total of twenty years, it implies that the proportion of women who can help relatives by participation in the market is pretty small.

4. If we compare the inter-age group differences in the relative significance of financial and non-financial reasons for participation, the youngest age-group of 25-34 turns out to be the only group present in the market solely on financial reasons. This corroborates our expectation of younger age group to be in need of finance more than the older age-groups. However, if we are to extend the category of younger age-group to cover up to 45-54 age-groups, the picture gets altered. Thus, we may as well say that there is a paradox in the sense that financial requirements are not necessarily more intense among the younger age-groups as compared to the older ones.

5. The non-financial reasons become an important factor for participation in the market as we cross the youngest age category. The desire to utilise time productively, and particularly to "remain young and live longer" as the women themselves put it, is an important non-financial reason for participation in the market. Overall, we may venture here to hypothesize the non-financial reasons as proxy variables representing the potential of the women to involve in socio-political issues.

Type of Family

We have seen the age-group-wise picture of the driving force of participation in the labour market. In this section, we shall be looking into the distribution of the main reasons by type of family.[11] Here we may mention the relative pressure of financial and non-

Table 4.3:Main Reasons for Employment by type of Family

Type of Family*	Financial reasons							Column VIII as the % of total number of vendors	Non-financial reasons							
	Economic pressure		Other economic needs		Higher standard of living		Total		Personaliy Traits		To utilize time		Traditional occupation		Total	
	Number	Percentage	Number	Percentage	Number	Percentage	Percentage		Number	Percentage	Number	Percentage	Number	Percentage		
I	II	III	IV	V	VI	VII	VIII	IX	X	XI	XII	XIII	XIV	XV	XVI	XVII
Separate	16	72.93	3	13.64	2	9.09	21 (95.46%)	7.00	1	4.54	-	-	-	-	1 (4.54%)	0.33
Joint	109	75.17	7	4.83	3	2.07	119 (82.07%)	39.67	4	2.76	20	13.79	2	1.38	26 (17.93%)	8.67
Nuclear	106	79.71	4	3	5	3.76	115 (86.47%)	38.33	2	1.5	15	11.28	1	0.75	18 (13.53%)	6.00

Source: Personal Survey

Note: The figures within parentheses are the percentages of the relevant row total.

* Nuclear family- Living with parents and children.
Joint family- Living with parents, sons, daughters, in-laws and grandchildren.
Separate family- Living with in-laws, children.

financial requirements for participation in the labour market according to the type of family.[12] While a vendor from nuclear or separate family could be, in the absence of family support system of the extended families, under bigger financial pressures, the joint families could as well be suffering from the same pressures due to the sheer size of the family and the well-known prevalence of shirking of responsibility in such family. This ambiguity in the case of financial reasons is not supposed to be so in the case of non-financial ones. Prima facie the non-financial reasons should be more pressing in the case of joint families than in separate or nuclear families primarily due to the larger number of family members in the former, other things remaining the same.[13]

Table 4.3 is the picture of the main reasons for employment by type of family as found in the survey. The major points emerging from the table are as follows:

1. As was seen earlier in the general scenario, financial reasons constitute the predominant reason for participation across family types. When we examine the financial reasons, no clear distinction emerges among the family types; the relative distribution on the basis of economic pressure alone gets altered when we look at the financial reasons as a whole. This could be just a reflection of the low level of socio-economic development of the land. Or there is need for more detailed scrutiny of the dynamics of financial and non-financial pressures across family types in Manipur.[14]
2. Non-financial reasons are, as expected, definitely stronger in nuclear and joint families than in separate families.
3. One feature which comes out glaringly from the table is the proportion of women in the market in order to utilise time. This is almost nil in the case of separate families but crosses 10 per cent in the case of nuclear and joint families. While a causal connection between tensions inside the family and the efforts of women to escape from the tensions cannot be established at this point, one cannot help wondering if there are active socio-economic tensions inside the families in Manipur, given the current level of economic development and the highly volatile socio-political milieu.

Table 4.4: Main Reasons for Employment by Marital Status

Marital Status	Financial reasons							Column VIII as the % of total number of vendors	Non-financial reasons							Column XVIas the % of total number of vendors
	Economic pressure		Other economic needs		Higher standard of living				Personality Traits		To utilize time		Traditional occupation			
	Number	Percent	Number	Percent	Number	Percent	Total		Number	Percent	Number	Percent	Number	Percent	Total	
I	II	III	IV	V	VI	VII	VIII	IX	X	XI	XII	XIII	XIV	XV	XVI	XVII
Unmarried	1	100	-	-	-	-	1 (100%)	0.33	-	-	-	-	-	-	-	0
Widow	70	83.33	4	4.77	3	3.57	77 (91.67%)	25.67	2	2.38	3	3.57	2	2.38	5 (8.33%)	2.33
Divorcee	3	42.86	2	28.57	-	-	5 (71.43%)	1.67	-	-	2	28.57	-	-	2 (28.57%)	0.67
Married	157	75.48	8	3.85	7	3.37	172 (82.7%)	57.33	5	2.4	30	14.42	1	0.48	36 (17.3%)	12

Source: Personal Survey

Note: The figures within parentheses are the percentages of the relevant row total.

Marital Status

We have seen the relative role of financial *vis-a-vis* non-financial reasons by age and type of family in accounting for the women participating in the labour force. In this section, we endeavour to examine the picture by marital status of the women in the market. In doing so, we follow the classification of women into unmarried, married, divorcee and widow.

Table 4.4 is a depiction of the women vendors in terms of their marital status and cause of work. While interpreting this table, we are ignoring the lone case of the unmarried as insufficient number of observation.[15]An examination of this table reveals the following picture:

1. The predominance of economic pressure among the widows (83.33 per cent) is well borne out by the table. This is reinforced by the relatively low proportion of widows (3.57 per cent) in the category participating in the labour force in order to utilise time; whereas a fairly high proportion of divorcee (28.57 per cent) followed by married women (14.42 per cent) do join the labour force to utilise time, this proportion is very low among the widows.[16]
2. We hazarded a guess about the familial tensions pushing women to join the labour force and thus utilise their time which would otherwise have been devoted to involvement in those tensions. This factor is probably strongest among the divorcees as exemplified by the nearly one-third (28.57 per cent) participating in the market in order to utilise time. This is followed by married women (14.42 per cent).
3. One distinct picture emerging from the table is the high proportion of divorcees (28.57 per cent) participating in the labour force on 'other economic needs'.[17] A detailed examination of this would take us into the foray of Psychological Economics.

Education

In this section, we endeavour to provide a picture of the driving forces of participation in the labour market by educational standards of the women.[18] The information is given in Table 4.5.

Table 4.5 throws up some interesting pictures about the main reasons for participation by educational status. While attempting to interpret the table, the illiterate group turned up a picture different from the trend observed in the case of the literates. In order to take account of this difference, we have regrouped the women into illiterates and literates. The following major pictures emerge from the table:

1. While overall the literate group displays the usual economic pressure (and ipso facto the financial reasons) as the predominant reason for participation, the importance of this declines as we go up the ladder of academic status. In fact, among the literates the importance of this factor (economic pressure) disappears at the level of the graduates.
2. The above trend among the literates gets reversed when it comes to non-financial reasons. As we go up the ladder of academic qualifications the proportion of women citing non-financial reasons as the force behind the participation rises; it rises from 10.31 per cent of the below matriculates to the entire proportion of above graduates citing this as the only reason. Within the non-financial reasons the proportion of graduates and above graduates joining the labour force in order to spend time is particularly interesting.
3. Among the illiterates, as in the case of others, financial reasons constitute the main reason for participation in the market. Among the non-financial reasons, the participation in the market in order to spend time displays more or less similar proportion as that of the below matriculates.

Size of Family

Studies of women's participation in the labour market mostly attempt to situate within the framework of empowerment and domestic violence.[19]

These studies on the women generally do not relate the findings to the respective size of the family.

Other things remaining the same, we should expect the role of women to be greater the larger the size of the family. This could be both in the sense of conventional household activities and in

Table 4.5: Main Reasons for Employment by Education

Educational Level		Financial reasons							Column VIII as the % of total number of vendors	Non-financial reasons							Column XVIas the % of total number of vendors
		Economic pressure		Other economic needs		Higher standard of living				Personality Traits		To utilize time		Traditional occupation			
		Number	Percent	Number	Percent	Number	Percent	Total		Number	Percent	Number	Percent	Number	Percent	Total	
I		II	III	IV	V	VI	VII	VIII	IX	X	XI	XII	XIII	XIV	XV	XVI	XVII
Illiterate	Illiterate	38	76	4	8	1	2	43 (86%)	14.33	2	4	5	10	0	0	7 (14%)	2.33
	Literate																
	Below Matri-culation	140	84.85	5	3.03	3	1.81	148 (89.69%)	49.33	2	1.22	15	9.09	0	0	17 (10.31%)	5.67
	Matri-culate	40	68.97	4	6.89	2	3.45	46	15.33 (79.31%)	1	1.72	9	15.52	2	3.45	12 (20.69%)	4.00
	Inter_ mediate	13	61.91	1	4.76	2	9.52	16 (76.19%)	5.33	2	9.53	3	14.28	0	0	5 (23.81%)	1.67
	Graduate	0	0	0	0	2	40	2 (40%)	0.67	0	0	2	40	1	20	3 (60%)	1.00
	Above •Graduate	0	0	0	0	0	0	0	0	0	0	1	100	0	0	1 (100%)	0.33
	Literate Total	193	80.01*	10	4.75*	9	12.37*	212	84.8	5	4.64*	30	15.84*	3	8.97*	38	15.2

Source: Personal Survey

Notes: 1. The figures within parentheses are the percentages of the relevant row total.

2. The asterisks (*) are percentages weighted by the relative proportions of the literate categories.

the sense of participation in the labour market. This responsibility could still be higher if the adults in the family are mostly female and the male members do not have opportunities for earning.

In any case, we should expect the size of the family to impact upon women's participation in the labour market and the reasons behind. In this section, we present a picture of the reasons for participation by size of the family to which each woman belongs. We give this picture in Table 4.6.

Some of the main features emerging from the table (Table 4.6) are as follows:

First, Economic Pressure, ipso facto financial reasons, as the main driving force for participation of the women in the labour market rises in prominence along with the rise in the size of the family. In other words, there is a synchronous relationship between the size of the family and women's participation in the labour market. The socio-economic implications of this are twofold: - (a) There is probably a rising and inescapable responsibility for women to earn along with the rise in the size of the family; and (b) Given the contemporary economic condition of the land, the employment opportunities of the male are not expanding in commensurate with the needs of the society. These factors might be pushing women more into the activities where there is little demand for modern technological inputs and the skill-content is relatively low.

Secondly, and in corollary to the first, the proportion of women participating in the labour market declines along with the rise in the size of the family. This inverse relationship reinforces the first positive relationship between size and participation.

Third, another interesting picture which emerges is the sharp decline in the proportion of women participating in the market to while away time as we go up the ladder of family size; this proportion declines from 33.33 per cent of the single member family to only 5.26 per cent of the large family. This as well strengthens the positive relationship between the size and the economic pressure.

Earners

The above analyses of the reasons for joining the labour

Table 4.6: Main Reasons for Employment by Size of Family

Size of Family	Financial reasons							Column VIII as the % of total number of vendors	Non-financial reasons							Column XVIas the % of total number of vendors
	Economic pressure		Other economic needs		Higher standard of living				Personality Traits		To utilize time		Traditional occupation			
	Number	Percent	Number	Percent	Number	Percent	Total		Number	Percent	Number	Percent	Number	Percent	Total	
I	II	III	IV	V	VI	VII	VIII	IX	X	XI	XII	XIII	XIV	XV	XVI	XVII
Single member	2	66.67	0	0	0	0	2 (66.67%)	0.67	0	0	1	33.33	0	0	1 (33.33%)	0.33
Small Family	87	69.05	5	3.97	3	2.38	95 (75.4%)	31.67	5	3.97	25	19.84	1	0.79	31 (24.6%)	10.33
Large Family	142	83.04	9	5.26	7	4.1	158 (92.4%)	52.67	2	1.17	9	5.26	2	1.17	13 (7.6%)	4.33

The figures within parentheses are the percentages of the relevant row total.

Source: Personal Survey

Note: Single family: A family living only one person either due to death of her husband or divorcee or their children got married.
Small family: A family having only one or two children.
Large family: A family having more than two children or who live jointly with uncle, aunt, or in- laws.

market is further pursued in this section by categorizing the women in the market by the number of earners in their respective families. For this exercise, we have adopted six categories as below:

A) Families in which the lone earning member is the woman;

B) Families in which there are two earning members including the woman;

C) Families in which there are three earning members including the woman;

D) Families in which there are four earning members including the woman;

E) Families in which there are five earning members including the woman; and

F) Families in which there are more than five earning members including the woman.

This exercise would give us a picture of the economic role of women at the micro level. In the empowerment literature, it is usually the earning status of the women which decides their fate.[20] So this analysis should give us an idea of economic empowerment of women at the micro level.

Further economic empowerment of women is generally highlighted in the literature of women studies as having positive effects on other aspects of familial and social existence. As such the micro picture which emerges would have implications for the decision making process. This issue is taken up later in the chapter.

While attempting to look deeply into the dynamics of socio-economic existence, it is important that we endeavour to appreciate the compulsions under which women participate in the labour market. Generally it is to be expected that the smaller the number of earners in the family the larger would be the economic and financial onus falling on the vendor women and vice-versa.

Still further, in Manipuri society the presence of women's market is considered as the mirror reflecting the social status of women. Whereas this could be true to the extent it goes, there is need to look at what is happening behind the mirror as well. The micro study would display pictures about the socio-economic health of the families and accordingly of the society. In this regard, the pre-eminence or otherwise of the economic and financial reasons determining the participation in the market would speak volumes.

With this background, the distribution of women on the basis of these six categories is given in Table 4.7.

The major pictures emerging from the table (Table 4.7) are:

1. It was seen in Table 4.6 that there are three single member families among the vendors. In the present table we see that there are one hundred and twenty-nine families (constituting 43 per cent of the total vendors in the market) in which there are only single earners, i.e., the women. After accounting for the three single member families, it implies that there are one hundred and twenty-six families (constituting 42 per cent of the total) where women in the market are the sole earning members. This category comprises the largest proportion of the women in the market. This, in fact, re-establishes the key economic role women play in the families of Manipur.

2. It is seen from the table that families having only one or two earning members constitute the largest proportion of the women in the market (61 per cent of the total). As expected, the economic and financial compulsions are the strongest forces pushing these women to the labour market. Again as expected the pre-eminence of the financial reasons gets reduced with the rise in the number of earners.

3. As regards the non-financial reasons for participation, three pictures are quite revealing. First, there is a positive association between the rise in the number of earners in the family and the pre-eminence of non-financial reasons. Secondly, after we cross the category of two earners per family, the intention to while away time by participation in the market rises sharply. Third, traditional occupation as a factor determining being present in the market is an important variable for the families having five earning members. In fact, for this particular category children upbringing and higher standard of living seem to be the driving force for whiling away time by participating in the traditional occupation.

Table 4.7: Main Reasons for Employment by Number of Earners

No. of Earners	Financial reasons: Economic pressure		Other economic needs		Higher standard of living			Column VIII as the % of total number of vendors	Non-financial reasons: Personality Traits		To utilize time		Traditional occupation			Column XVIas the % of total number of vendors
	Number	Percent	Number	Percent	Number	Percent	Total		Number	Percent	Number	Percent	Number	Percent	Total	
I	II	III	IV	V	VI	VII	VIII	IX	X	XI	XII	XIII	XIV	XV	XVI	XVII
1	125	96.90	0	0	2	1.55	127 (98.45%)	42.33	0	0	2	1.55	0	0	2 (1.55%)	0.67
2	50	80.64	2	3.23	4	6.46	56 (90.33%)	18.67	1	1.62	5	8.05	0	0	6 (9.67%)	02
3	33	56.90	8	13.80	2	3.45	43 (74.15%)	14.33	2	3.45	12	20.68	1	1.72	15 (25.85%)	05
4	21	50	2	4.76	1	2.38	24 (57.14%)	08	4	9.52	13	30.95	1	2.38	18 (42.85%)	06
5	0	0	2	33.33	1	16.67	3 (50%)	01	0	0	2	33.33	1	16.67	3 (50%)	01
5+	0	0	0	0	0	0	0	0	0	0	3	100	0	0	3 (100%)	01

The figures within parentheses are the percentages of the relevant row total.

Source: Personal Survey

From Earning to Empowerment

In the light of the above findings and the main issues highlighted in the literature on women studies, it would be in place to put the distinguishing features found in Manipur here. In the literature, it is emphasized that the very fact of earning an independent income gives women an opportunity to reduce their economic dependence on men and increase their 'centrality' within the household (Arunachalam and Kalpagam, 2007). This has been found to be true even in cases where the women's contribution to household income is low. What we have found in the case of Manipur are two-fold. First, women do join in the labour market mainly for economic reasons. Secondly, in a large majority of the cases, the income contribution of the women is significant at the household level and thus important at the economy-wide level.

Further, it is also emphasized in the literature that earning an independent income increases the bargaining power of women at the household level and enhances autonomy while at the same time reducing their traditional seclusion. What we find in the case of Manipur is the absence of such seclusion as evidenced from the historical participation of women in political, economic and social activities.

Thus, a priori we find situations in Manipur which would be the envy of any empowerment-protagonist of women. Given this background it would be rewarding both theoretically and empirically as to how this large scale economic participation as well as contribution of women in Manipur translates into actual empowerment outcomes.

Why the need of Empowerment of Women?

Regarding empowerment of women, A.P.J. Abdul Kalam, former President of India, emphatically wrote: "Empowering women is a prerequisite for creating a good nation, when women are empowered, society with stability is assured. Empowerment of women is essential as their thoughts and their value systems lead to the development of a good family, good society and ultimately a good nation."[21] Now there are observers who plead for empowering women in order to usher into a "*safer world*".[22]

Empowerment of Women has been defined by different scholars in different ways; it is as if there are as many definitions as there are women scholars.[23] But in the main it includes the following components:[24]

1. Enable women fight their own fears and feeling of inadequacy and inferiority.
2. Making them economically independent and self-reliant at both the individual and the household level.
3. Creating and strengthening women's groups and organisations at the societal level.
4. Establishing gender equality in terms of opportunities for employment and social mobility.
5. Valuing and promoting qualities of nurturing, caring and gentleness, values usually identified with women, in social interactions.
6. Ensure access, control over and benefit of resources like capital, land, property and technology to women.
7. Reducing women's burden of work especially within home.

At this point, we must hasten to add that empowerment of women is both a process and a product. It is a process in the sense that certain changes in social norms and institutions are fundamental to establish conditions fulfilling the components of empowerment mentioned above. It is a product as well in the sense that fulfilling of the conditions as a result of the changes enables women to perform social roles more meaningfully and effectively.

Empowerment of Women Vendors

Given the brief exposition on empowerment given above and the analyses on participation in the labour market, an attempt is made in what follows to assess the extent and depth of empowerment among the women vendors in the Khwairamband Keithel. For the purposes of our analysis, the empowerments realized or otherwise through employment are examined in terms of the following five elements:[25]

1. Economic Contribution
2. Economic Independence
3. Participation and Autonomy in Decision-making
4. Participation in Political Activities
5. Remaining Contemporary and Relevant

1. Economic Contribution

Economic contribution by women has direct as well as derived implications. It results in an increase in the security and welfare of the entire household. Such contribution can change the lives of women and their families, and raise the overall standard of living of the household. Further the contribution enables women to effect enhanced spending on themselves; this is taken as an improvement of their status within the household. It also reflects an empowered state of being for the women, as it brings forth a sense of self-worth and self-esteem through a perceived self-interest.[26] Sen describes this as a change in women's self-perception, an aspect which is the slowest and hardest to change, as it involves a process of internal confrontation with issues dealing with their subordinate position within the household.[27]

In order to ascertain the extent of economic contribution of women vendors to the economic corpus of their respective households, we have categorized the vendors according to their level of contribution per week. We have adopted six categories defined by a range of Rs.300 between any two adjacent categories. The picture which emerges is tabulated in Table 4.8.

A. The proportion of women who contributed up to Rs 300 per week forms the largest proportion with 23.33 per cent and women who contribute Rs 1501 and above constitute the least proportion with only 6 per cent. Women whose economic contribution is within Rs 301-600 and Rs 901-1200 each per week to their family have a share of about 16 percent each.

B. It was stated in the beginning of the book that poverty has a woman's face. One prominent picture emerging from the table is the significant role women play in enabling their respective households in escaping from poverty, *ceteris paribus*. Even the lowest contributing category of 23 per cent would enable

Table 4.8: Economic Contribution by Women Vendors per Week/Year

Categories	*Amount (in Rs.)*		*Number*	*Percentage Distribution*
	Week	*Year**		
I	Up to 300	Up to 15,600	70	23.33
II	301 – 600	15,652 – 31,200	47	15.67
III	601 – 900	31,252 – 46,800	65	21.67
IV	901 – 1,200	46,852 – 62,400	48	16
V	1,201-1,500	62,452 – 78,000	52	17.33
VI	1,501 and above	78,052 and above	18	6
	Total		300	100

* The data collected were on weekly contribution. The yearly figures have been derived by multiplying the weekly figure by the number of weeks in a year, assuming that the vendors work for all the days in a year. This is not an unrealistic assumption because they would not be in the market only when absolutely unavoidable circumstances, like death or accident of relatives and such unavoidable compulsions, arise.

Source: Personal Survey

their households to remain at least around the poverty line, and, in fact, this would enable the households to escape from poverty with a limited contribution from the other members of the households. If we club the categories up to Rs. 900, the proportion of households escaping poverty more or less solely on the strength of the women's contributions is more than half of the total.

C. If we relate Table 4.8 with the information on business hours given in Section 3.8.1.8,a clear picture emerges on how women allocate their time in order that the respective families escape poverty. A combined reading of the two establishes that the women vendors devote substantial hours of work to market activities by necessity, not by choice,[28]to provide a non-poverty standard of living and thereby allowing themselves minimal licence to rest and recreation.

D. We can also have a more meaningful macroeconomic picture of the economic contribution of the women vendors if we situate their contribution within the overall household income of a family. In order to perform this exercise, we have taken the

Net State Domestic Product of Manipur (NSDP) for the year 2005-06 (Rs. 5,120 crore),[29] for which we have final data. We have taken the data on the number of households of Manipur (3,84,199)[30]from the 2001 Census of India. When we divide the NSDP by the number of households the per household income per year works out to Rs.1,33,264. When we examine the contribution of vendors as a proportion of this household income, the share ranges from about 12 per cent of the up to Rs. 300 category to 59 per cent of the Rs. 1501 and above category.

2. Economic Independence

In the previous section we have seen how extensive the contributions of women vendors are to the economic maintenance of their respective families. To the extent that these are significant the women have been empowered. The depth of this empowerment, however, remains to be examined in the sense that we need to ascertain how far the contributions get translated into economic independence of the women themselves.

This examination of the economic independence or otherwise of the women vendors is significant because dependence has been found to be the villain who makes women powerless. When the husband is the sole earning member of a family, the woman [wife] has perforce to depend upon him, even for very personal and petty expenses. Since such occasions are more frequent than not, the husband continually gets an opportunity to remind her of her dependence on him and his authority over her. This binding constraint of women is solved forever, once they start to earn. Having an independent income has been found to generate three positive effects:- (a)increase their [women] self-reliance;(b) reduce their dependency on household income; and (c) help them to stand on their feet.[31]

At this point it is incumbent on our part to attempt defining what we mean by the term *economic independence*. We can think of someone as economically independent if she has resources of her own, whether inherited or earned, which she can spend on items she desires and she gets utility out of it. In the absence of inheritance, she can attain such level only when she is able to have some savings of her own out of her earnings and after having met the unavoidable expenses. Thus the level of savings of a woman would, *ceteris paribus*, indicate the depth of economic independence or otherwise generally termed as economic self-reliance. In other words, own savings would generate, other things remaining the same, the three positive effects, viz.,(a) increase their [women] self-reliance; (b) reduce their dependency on household income; and (c) help them to stand on their feet, mentioned in the previous paragraph.

Accordingly, we have taken savings of the women vendors as the prima facie indicator of their level of economic independence.[32] For convenience of analysis and clarity of understanding, we have divided the women vendors into six categories by their level of monthly savings by adopting a range of Rs. 300. The picture emerging from this grouping is given in Table 4.9.

Table 4.9: Amounts Saved in a Month

Categories	*Amount*	*Number*	*Percentage Distribution*
I	Up to 300	51	17.00
II	301-600	40	13.33
III	601-900	56	18.67
IV	901-1200	87	29.00
V	1201-1500	34	11.33
VI	1501 and above	32	10.67
Total		*300*	*100*

Source: Personal Survey

The prominent pictures emerging from Table 4.9 are given below:

A. The most prominent picture is the fact of every woman saving some amount or the other out of their earnings. This speaks volumes about the economic acumen of the women vendors, particularly so because their participation in the labour market was driven by economic reasons. Further, we must also recall that the size of business was small in most cases. The significance of this financial acumen is enhanced when we notice that the women vendors have the habit of maintaining their saving either by joining *marup*[33] or depositing in private micro-finance institutions[34]. This implies that the women have understood the power of economic empowerment and the significance of economic independence.

B. Secondly, it is seen that 49 per cent of the total saved an amount of Rs. 900 or less per month. In other words, this amount serves as the half-line dividing the women into two halves, one below and another above.

C. The largest proportion of women in the savings level is found in the category of those who save between Rs. 901 and Rs. 1,200 per month. In fact, if we combine this with the proportion belonging to the Rs. 601-900, the proportion comes to about 48 per cent of the total.

D. The last two highest categories taken together constitute a little over one-fifth of the total.

3. *Participation and Autonomy*[35]*in the Decision-making at the Household Level*

This section purports to examine the issue of participation and autonomy in decision-making of the women at the household level. In the previous two sections, we have seen the extent and the depth of economic empowerment of the women vendors. It was established that they are definitely empowered on this score. This economic empowerment, however, would not bear the expected fruits[36] for the women unless it is accompanied by participation and autonomy in decision-making at both household and societal levels. While the societal aspects would be taken up in the subsequent sections, the household issue is examined here.

When it comes to decision-making, intra-familial relationships between the spouses is seen as bargaining based on power relations, conscious or albeit.[37] The situation ranges from total exclusion from decision-making to fair participation. In all these, the income-status of the women has been found to be the crucial determining factor.[38] So, it becomes important to examine if the economic empowerment of women vendors is accompanied by a concomitant strength in the bargaining position of the very women.

In order to delve into these aspects of decision-making at the familial level, we collected information into seven crucial areas of household decision-making in so far as they relate to the women vendors. The seven areas relate to decision-making on

(i) Children's education
(ii) Joining the labour market
(iii) Savings from current earnings
(iv) Food purchase
(v) Medical treatment
(vi) Purchases of clothing; and
(vii) Recreation.

Of these seven areas, I and IV are mainly family-wide matters, while V and VII are fundamentally personal matters. In the remaining three, the family-wide and personal matters are intertwined. As per the definition of autonomy given in footnote bearing number 162, we may think of II and VII as relating to freedom of mobility whereas participation is relevant for all the seven areas. A picture of the relative participation in decision-making on these seven areas is given in Table 4.10.

The broad scenario emerging from Table 4.10 are as follows:

A. As expected and desirable, the extra-familial influence is near non-existent in all the seven areas of decision-making. Whatever little presence of external participation in decision-making, which is reflected in the table, is naturally expected in the case of any family in social context.

B. The most prominent area which establishes autonomy of the women in decision-making turns out to be saving from current earning. Of the seven variables, this happens to be the only one where the number of self-decision on the matter is larger than that of other categories. If we add to this category the number of joint decision makers, the proportion of women vendors playing role in saving decisions is more than sixty per cent of the total. This reflects the economic acumen and the concern for personal self-resilience of the women. This is so because savings ultimately are the factors which would provide them security in both good and bad times.

Table 4.10: Percentage Distribution of Women Vendors' by Participation and Autonomy in Decision-making at Household Level

Category	Household Matters	Self	Husband	Joint (Vendor and her Husband)	Others	Total
I	Children's education	55 (18.52 %)	150 (50.51%)	90 (30.30%)	2 (0.67%)	297* (100%)
II	Joining the labour market	90 (30%)	133 (43.33%)	67 (22.33%)	10 (3.33%)	300 (100%)
III	Saving from current earning	121 (40.33%)	116 (38.67%)	60 (20%)	3 (1%)	300 (100%)
IV	Food purchase	84 (28%)	154 (51.33%)	60 (20%)	2 (0.67%)	300 (100%)
V	Medical treatment	53 (17.67%)	159 (53%)	83 (27.67%)	5 (1.66%)	300 (100%)
VI	Purchases of clothing	91 (30.33%)	134 (44.67%)	70 (23.33%)	5 (1.66%)	300 (100%)
VII	Recreation	51 (17%)	149 (49.67%)	90 (30%)	10 (3.33%)	300 (100%)

*One is unmarried and another two have no children.

Source: Personal Survey

Note: The figures within parentheses are the percentages of the relevant row total.

C. Other than the savings decisions, the proportion of husbands deciding on the issue is higher than that of the women themselves in all the decision areas. Nevertheless we need to select out decisions to work, food purchase and clothing as areas where women do play a significant role in decision-making, particularly so if we take the jointly decided ones as well into account.

D. Medical treatment, recreation and children's education are areas where the dominant decision takers are invariably the husbands.

From the examination of the scenario as detailed above two parallel interpretations can be arrived at. If we look at the savings decisions only the earlier picture of economic empowerment acquires the necessary depth. However, we cannot be so sure about empowerment in the other areas of familial decision-making, which seemingly reduces the depth and strength of the economic empowerment. In other words, along with the economic empowerment, there appears to be a weakening, if not reversal, of empowerment in non-economic areas of household decision-making. We would call this scenario "Empowerment Paradox".[39] In terms of the definition of autonomy adopted here, we can say that though there are strong signals of autonomy yet there are still areas where this has to be firmly established.[40]

4. Participation in Political Activities

The above three components of empowerment we have examined relate mainly to individual and familial levels. In this section, we look into the perspective and involvement of the women in political processes. This section, to put it another way, delves into the involvement of the women in the societal component of empowerment.

In order to examine this societal aspect of empowerment, we collected information on two aspects. The first aspect relates to participation in the electoral process, while the second one relates to participation in organisations[41] (in the sense of clubs). While collecting information on the questions relating to political participation and based on the structured questionnaire, some powerful comments emerged spontaneously from the women. These comments reflect strong organisational commitment for social causes. It would be in place to recall some of these with a view to enhance our understanding of structured information collected. While discussing on the role of decision-makers, almost three-fourths of the women supported the necessity of having women in this positions as they understand own problems better.

A very strong sentiment which cuts across all the women vendors is the appreciation of the necessity for organisation. It has been articulated as the medium and the power to address individual as well as collective problems of existence. The urge and commitment to participate in organisations for collective action is evident even from the not-so-active members when they rationalise their non-active participation as organisational lapses[42] rather than dispensing with the need for organisation as such.

Those active in organisations are very vocal about the positive effects of these. Among them, fish, vegetables and clothes vendors are particular about knowledge-sharing experience, strength of unity, breaking of isolation and problem-solving effects of organisations. Some even speak of organisation as providing the power to independently articulate and work for social cause, particularly in so far as it serves women's interests. In the process organisation provides women to open up with each other with their personal problems, which otherwise they feel inhibited to tell anyone.

5. Participation in Electoral Process

With this general understanding of the psychological orientation of the women vendors towards organising themselves in group, we shall now go back to examining the two aspects of societal empowerment. In this, we take up the issue of political participation[43] first. Perhaps because of the historical dominance of political arena by men as kings and soldiers, women have generally been considered as 'naturally' unsuitable for political activity. This general perception has been the factor behind formal and informal exclusion of women from political activities. In India the political gender gap has been found to be particularly wide.[44]

In a democracy, election of representatives is the most important political process. We have enquired if the women exercise their franchise or not, and the rationale for their action. A picture of this is given in Table 4.11.

The inherent political consciousness and the awareness for participation among the women are well evident from the discussion on organisation above. This is unambiguously corroborated by the data depicted in table 4.11. Responses on whether exercised the franchise or not in the electoral process were collected. The major pictures emerging from the table 4.11 are:

A. The most telling scene emerging from the table is the extraordinarily high proportion of women exercising the right

Table 4.11: Percentage Distribution of Women Vendors' by Participation in Electoral Process

Participation in Electoral Process	*Number*	*Reasons*	*Number*
Voting	298 (99.33%)	a) For upliftment of their society and to raise the standard of women	206 (69.13%)
		a) Everyone votes	21 (7.05%)
		b) Right to vote	54 (18.11%)
		c) To promote a party	17 (5.71%)
Not voting	2 (0.67%)	a) Do not trust the politician leaders	2 (0.67%)
Total			*300 (100%)*

Source: Personal Survey

to vote in the electoral process. The proportion of 99.33 per cent participating in the voting process is high in both absolute and relative terms. Since there is no proportion as high as this one among any other category of the electorates, we can unequivocally state that women in the market possess a deep sense of political participation unseen in other population categories. We cannot, in the absence of time series data, make a definitive statement on the level of political awareness. We can, however, infer that this level could be a historical fact, given the active involvement of women of this market in all the epochal women's movements we mentioned in Chapter Two.

B. The level of participation gains much more significance if we examine further the reasons for participation into the voting process. A proportion close to as high as three-fourths express social upliftment and advancement of women as the prime reason for participation in the voting process. This again could be an inherent and inherited characteristic of the women in

Table 4.12: Distribution of Vendors by Membership of Women Organization, Participation in Agitation and Meira Paibi[47]

Member of Women Organization				*Participation in Agitation*				*Member of Meira Paibi*			
Yes		*No*		*Yes*		*No*		*Yes*		*No*	
Number	*Percentage*	*Number*	*Percentage*	*Number*	*Percentage*	*Number*	*Percentage*	*Number*	*Percentage*	*Number*	*Percentage*
240	80	60	20	299	99.67	1	0.33	207	69	93	31

Source: Personal Survey

the market if we recall the causes which sparked women's agitations in the twentieth century[45] and even beyond.

C. That this level of participation and commitment is deep rooted is also indirectly confirmed when only 7 per cent of the women state following others as the reason for participation in voting.

Overall we can confidently speak of the commitment to the political process and the expectation for improvement from the pictures emerging while examining their political participation.

Participation in Organisation

Whereas the reasons for organisational participation and commitment to social cause have been seen earlier, this section purports to see the level of participation in organisation. It was noted in Chapter Two that women of Manipur would rise against any social injustice and gross violation of human rights. The accuracy of this general observation is well brought out by the information contained in Table 4.12, which provides percentage distribution of vendors by level of participation in organisational activities.

The following pictures eminently emerge from Table 4.12.

A. Almost 80 per cent of the women are members of one or the other organisation of women.

B. The most interesting and powerfully revealing picture of Table 4.12 is the absolute participation in agitations as stated by the women themselves. This confirms the historically established orientation of the market women playing leading role in issues of social concerns.

C. It was seen that the celebrated Meira Paibi movements in Manipur are spearheaded by middle-aged and older women. This fact is also established by the responses reproduced in table 4.12. It is seen that as high as 69 per cent of the women are members of Meira Paibi organisations in their respective localities. The remaining 31 per cent are mostly the younger members of the vendors, and the elder members of their families usually take part in Meira Paibi activities.

By way of summarizing the implications of this section, we may say that women vendors' life in the political activities is about "boldness"- the boldness to face their daily existence, their community and to confront the fear of injustice and oppression. This is made possible through their participation in political activities that help to build up solidarity and boldness. This quality greatly enhances their self-respect and gives every woman a sense of dignity as an individual. This, along with the collective action,[46] improves articulation, generates power to overcome obstacles and achieve their objectives, hence reflecting their empowerment.

5. Remaining Contemporary and Relevant

From Chapter Two and the previous section, we have seen the historical and contemporary involvement of the women in moments of critical social crisis. This has become as almost the second nature of the women in the market in as much as all of them reported participation in socio-political agitations as and when the circumstances demanded. But this level of involvement can be effective and meaningful only when founded on a strong information based. In fact, the dictum of information as power is truly applicable in this case.

Information through the various means of mass media empowers women to the extent it makes them aware of the various issues, challenges and happenings around the world. When women are informative they can take advantage of opportunities, access services, exercise their rights, negotiate effectively, and can hold state and non-state actors accountable. Timely access to information by various means is particularly important for the women to empower themselves.[48]

In the light of the above background, we examine whether women vendors had independent information from the media or through other means to empower themselves.

One can gather information on public affairs from various sources. We have classified the sources into six categories depending on the nature of information provision, viz., newspaper, radio, television, customer, peers and others. A picture of the relative distribution of women by use of media as source of information is given in Table 4.13.

Table 4.13: Distribution of Women Vendors' by Use of Media

Category	*Medium of Information*	*Number*	*Percentage Distribution*
I	By reading newspaper	62	20.67
II	By listening to radio	72	24
III	By watching television	113	37.67
IV	Asking the customer	3	1
V	From peers	50	16.66
VI	Others	–	–
	Total	300	100

Source: Personal Survey

The major points emerging from Table 4.13 are:

A. In recent years television has emerged as arguably the most powerful medium of information transmission. This is also visible among the women vendors as the largest proportion depends on this medium as the source of information.

B. The three important sources of information are newspaper, radio and television. This is also true in the case of women in the market. Besides these three sources of information, the other important source is peer group interaction.

Conclusion

The historical strength of active participation of Manipuri women in society-wide issues still continues. It is as if the understanding of the important role that participation in outside the household economic activities can play in ameliorating living conditions has almost become generic to the women of Manipur, particularly so among the women vendors. This predominance of the economic factor can be both contextual as determined by the socio-economic situation of the society and personal as determined by the household level of well-being. A socio-politically more significant factor is the commitment of the women in the market to involve in organisations for collective cause as evident from the various historical movements for societal causes; this also could be a continuation of the inherent feature of the Manipuri women. This orientation for collective engagement for social responsibility gets reflected in the extraordinarily high level of participation in the electoral process. While more research is needed for understanding empowerment of the Manipuri women within the household decision-making process, their political-economic empowerment at the macro level is invariably seen.

NOTES & REFERENCES

1. An interview with Amar Yumnam, Director, Centre for Manipur Studies, Professor, Department of Economics, Manipur University, Dated, 22nd September 2009.
2. In the sense of New Economic Geography, wherein geography, widely defined, has been emphasized as a deep determinant of the development process. See for instance Ottaviano, Gianmarco I. P. and Jacques-Francois Thisse, (2004), *New Economic Geography: What About the N?*, Mimeo., September; and Fujita, Masahisa and Tomoya Mori, (2005), *Frontiers of the New Economic Geography,* Institute of Developing Economies, Discussion Paper No. 27, April.
3. ILO, An International Survey of the Conditions of Working Women with Home and Family Responsibilities, as mentioned in Myrdal, Alva and Viola Klein, (1962), *Women's Two Roles,* Routledge and Kegan Paul, London, pp.82.
4. Cf. the institution of Lallup Kaba and the consequent participation of women in economic activities outside the household.
5. Government of India, (1964), "International Trends", *Women in Employment,* Labour Bureau, Ministry of Labour and Employment, pp. 58-59.
6. Joshi, S. C., (2004), Chapter 2 in *Women Empowerment: Myth and Reality,* Akansha Publishing House, New Delhi, pp 14-30.
7. Here we may recall our earlier two findings reflected in the previous chapter. First, the economic motive for joining in the business was well borne. Secondly, the predominance of low scale vendors was also established.
8. We shall have more to say on the relationship of this with the empowerment position of women later in the chapter.
9. Similar findings are reported by Bhadra, C., (2007), *International Labour Migration of Nepalese Women: Impact of their Remittances on Poverty Reduction,* Asia-Pacific Research and Training Network

on Trade, Working Paper, Series No. 44; and Klien, V., (1965), *Britain's Married Women Workers*, Routledge and Kegan Paul, London, pp. 36-37. The conflict between family life and work of women is now an important area of research.

We are not touching upon this issue in this book. However, for a general discussion on this issue, see, Calvert, E., Russell, H., O'Connell, P., and McGinnity, F.,(2009), *Reconciling Work and Family life: Workplaces, Occupation and the Experience of Work Life Conflict*, Economic and Social Research Institute, Dublin, Ireland, Research Bulletin 2009/3/4.

10. Death of male bread earners, particularly among younger adults of the family, could be one such reason.
11. The family type we adopt here is the same as was adopted in Section 3.8.1.4.
12. A clear picture on this cannot be established a priori.
13. There is a saying in Manipuri, which literally translated means: "More mouth to feed, less hands to work with".
14. This, however, is beyond the scope of the present exercise.
15. Even though this case was purely random as the vendors were surveyed on the basis of random selection from the different market sheds.
16. This calls for detailed examination of the relative socio-economic dynamics of the different categories of marital status. This, however, is not a theme of enquiry in the present research.
17. That is to help relatives and to meet personal health expenses. For details of the classifications, see Table 4.1.
18. The classification of the vendors by educational level follows the one adopted in Section 3.8.1.2.
19. For a recent study in this regard, see, Bhattacharya, M., Bedi, S. A., and Chhachhi, A. , (2009),

    Marital Violence and Women's Employment and Property Status: Evidence from North Indian Villages, IZA, *Discussion Paper No. 4361*, August and the references given therein.
20. In the empowerment literature, greatest emphasis is put on market participation as a determinant of the level of empowerment. Further the recent focus on micro finance in the policy realm founds its rationale on the power of economic factors in explaining

empowerment. One may refer, inter alia, Duflo, E. (2003). 'Grandmothers and Granddaughters: Old Age Pension and Intra-Household Allocation in South Africa'. *World Bank Economic Review*, Vol. 42, pp. 1-25; Narayan, D., with Patel, R., Schafft, K., Rademacher, A., and Koch-Schulte, S., (2000), *Voices of the Poor: Can Anyone Hear Us?*, Oxford University Press, New York.

21. As quoted by Yadav, R. P., Raginideep and Roy, P., (2008), Empowerment of Women in India in Pandhya, R., (2008), ed., *Women Welfare and Empowerment in India-Vision for 21st Century*, (2008), New Century Publication, New Delhi, p.341.

22. Potts, M., Hayden. T., (2008), *Sex and War: How Biology Explains Warfare and Terrorism and Offers a Path to a Safer World*, Benbella Books, Dallas.

23. Definitions of empowerment reveal both diversity and commonality. Most of the definitions focus mainly on the issues of gaining power and control over decisions and resources that affects the quality of one's own life. See, for example, Rozario, (2002), Mujeri, M.K., (2002), Mukhyopadhya and Sudarshan, (2003). Most also take into account structural inequalities that affect the entire social groups rather than focusing on individual characteristics. See, for example, World Bank, (1995), UNICEF, (2001), UNDP, (1995). In an extensive exploration of the term empowerment, Kabeer (1999, 2001) focuses on three dimensions that define the capacity to exercise strategic life choices: access to resources, agency, and outcomes. Amartya Sen (1985, 1999) has written extensively on the importance of substantive freedoms and the individual freedom to choose and achieve different outcomes.

24. Yadav. R.P., Raginideep and Roy. p., (2008), *op. cit.*, p. 345.

25. C.f. Claros, A. L., and Zahidi. S., (2005), Women's Empowerment: Measuring the Global Gender Gap, *World Economic Forum*, Geneva.

26. About the importance of individual income to the economic role of women, See, for example, Kabeer and Mahmud, (2004), "Globalization, Gender and Poverty: Bangladesh Women Workers in Export and Local Market", *Journal of International Development*, Vol. 16, No.1, pp. 93-109.

27. Sen, (1999), *op.cit.*, p. 257.

28. About women who work long hours 'by choice', one may refer, Goodin, R., Rice, M. J., Parpo A., and Eriksson, L., (2008), *Discretionary Time: A New Measure of Freedom*, Cambridge University Press, Cambridge.

29. Ministry of Finance, *Economic Survey*- 2007-08, Government of India, Table A-12.
30. Publications of the Office of the Registrar General, India as given in *Statistical Abstract Manipur*, 2007, Table 4.1.
31. Kabeer, N. and Mahmud,S., (2004), Globalization, Gender and Poverty: Bangladesh Women Workers in Export and Local Market, *Journal of International Development*, Vol. 16, pp. 93 – 109.
32. There is legitimacy in taking savings as the indicator as these are made out of the actual own earnings of the women from their participation in the labour market.
33. The literal meaning of the Manipuri word "MARUP" is friend. However, in the present context a marup means a financial institution whose primary objective is to periodically form a substantial amount of money by way of recurring subscriptions from among friends and acquaintances who work on mutual understanding and good will. These friends and acquaintances are called members of the Marup. Perhaps the term Marup meaning friend has been adopted for such a body as it is organized by friends and acquaintances. The fund so realized periodically is given to a member called a winner. The winner is chosen either by lot or by negotiation and this process of choosing a winner is called a draw. For every period a winner is chosen. A period may be a month, a week or even a day. Generally a past winner contributes a certain nominal amount over and above the usual subscription. As a result every subsequent winner gets an extra sum equal to the total amount of additional contribution from all the previous winners. A marup with a certain number of members is said to have completed its life when every member becomes a winner by turns.
34. About private micro-finance institutions, one can refer Section 3.8.1.9. It was also found during the survey that that the women vendors prefer to deposit their small earnings in private micro-finance institutions than by joining marup as they suggest that the micro-finance institutions were sounder institutions and could imply easier access to credit in case of crisis as well as for business.
35. Autonomy has been variously defined as "the ability to obtain information and to use it as the basis of making decisions about one's private concerns and those of one's intimates" (Dyson and Moore 1983: 45); and "the degree of women's access to (and control over) material resources (including food, income, land, and other forms of wealth) and to social resources (including knowledge, power, and prestige) within the family, in the community, and in the society

at large" (Dixon 1978: 6). We define autonomy here as freedom of mobility and participation in household decision making.

36. Generally an earner is expected to exercise her liberty on selecting the items of expenditure. Even within the familial context of shared and collective responsibilities, the earner is expected to have a significant say in household decision-making.

37. See Pandolfelli, L., Meinzen-Dick, R., and Dohrn, S., (2007), Gender and Collective Action: A Conceptual Framework for Analysis, Paper presented at the International Research Workshop on '*Gender and Collective Action*' October, 17-21, 2005, Chiang Mai, Thailand, CAPRi, Working Paper No. 64, International Food Policy Research Institute, and the references given in the paper.

38. See, Blau, F. D., (1998), "Trends in the Well-being of American Women," *Journal of Economic Literature*, Vol.36, No.1, pp. 112-165; and Rahman, L., and Rao. V., (2004), The Determinants of Gender Equity in India: Examining Dyson and Moore's Book with New Data, *Population and Development Review*, Vol. 30, No. 2, pp. 239-268.

39. Cf. Kabeer opines that unequal decision making in the family is due to women's "time poverty". See, Kabeer, N., (2003), *Gender Mainstreaming in Poverty Eradication and the Millennium Development Goals*, Commonwealth Secretariat, London. Since our research has a limited purpose, it will be interesting and rewarding if we examine the reasons for unequal decision making in the family, but it is beyond the scope of our present book. Also compare Sather and Kazi's (1997) findings in rural areas of the Pakistani Punjab where women are consulted in all decisions, either domestic or economic, but do not act as major decision-makers. Sather, Z. and S. Kazi, (1997), *Women's Autonomy, Livelihood and Fertility: A Case of Rural Punjab*, Pakistan Institute of Development Economics, Islamabad.

40. There could be psycho-social factors in play here besides purely economic ones. The examination of these is, however, lie outside the domain of the present exercise. Besides, the ultimate answer to the issue can be provided only by panel data studies.

41. There was no specificity on the concept while collecting information. But in the context of Manipur, these could mean from locality level groups for specific causes to State-level political wings of various political parties.

42. Some of the lapses they point out are infrequent interactions through

meetings, non-listening to the issues they raise, etc.

43. In conventional analysis, political participation means activities related to electoral politics like voting, campaigning, holding party office and contesting election. But in broader sense it encompasses all voluntary actions intended to influence the making of public policies, the administration of public affairs and the choice of political leaders at all levels of government. Political interventions by women of India today range from movement for peace and good governance to protest against dowry, rape, domestic violence, food adulteration, price rise etc. See Desai, N. and Thakkar, U., (2007), "Women and Political Participation in India", *Women in Indian Society*, National Book Trust, New Delhi.

44. There exists a large gender gap in political empowerment in India. See Nayak, P., and Mahanta, B., (2009), Women Empowerment in India, MPRA Paper No. 12685; and *World Economic Forum*, India Gender Gap Report, 2009, Geneva.

45. See Chapter 2.

46. About the impact of collective action on gender equity and women's empowerment, one may refer, Kabeer, N., (1994), Reversed Realities: Gender Hierarchies in Development Thought, Verso, London; and Pandolfelli, L., Meinzen-Dick, R., Dohrn, S., (2007), Gender and Collective Action: A Conceptual Framework for Analysis, Collective Action and Property Rights (CAPRi), *Working Paper No. 64*.

47. See Section 2.8.3.

48. For a more detailed discussion on access to information and women empowerment, please refer, Narayan, D., *et al.,* (2002), *Empowerment and Poverty Reduction, Poverty Reduction and Economic Management,* (PREM), World Bank, Washington, D.C. One can also refer, Narayan, D. and Shah, T., (2000), *Connecting the Local to the Global: Voices of the Poor*, World Bank, Washington, D.C.

5

Conclusion

We are in an epoch when women studies are gaining increasing importance both theoretically and empirically. In the beginning, there were more of air and heat, and less of light. But in the last two to three decades, there has undergone a tremendous change in the subject. Besides scholars with different disciplinary backgrounds, the subject is now the focus of all the significant international bodies. As a result of this, the subject is now marked more by light and substance with the areas needing further research more clearly defined.

One finding which has emerged powerfully from these studies is the prevalence of women's face in poverty. In this context the necessity is being emphasized of enhancing the social, economic and political position of women through multiple approaches for equalization of opportunities. Given the global scenario of research, there is need for appreciating the picture of Manipur with the objective of identifying the similarities and the differences.

The geo-political location of Manipur at the intersection of South, South-east and East Asia has made it a melting pot of waves of people and their cultures. This necessarily has provided the women of the land with certain unique features. These features are rewarding areas for studies on women.

Some of these features have stood the test of history. Women of Manipur have been active in business related activities right from the pre-colonial to the post-colonial times of today. This has been coupled by the opportune and necessary involvements in movements for social, political and economic justice from time to time. The relative equi-proportionality of the size of men and women in the population has been a stable feature of the population right from the pre-colonial times. Though female literacy was understandably low in the beginning i.e., the end of the 19th century, it has been rising continuously though still below the male literacy rate. In fine, the confirmatory and the impactful role of women in the socio-politico-economic process of the State has been salient since long. The issue of concern, however, remains the lack of appropriate participation in formal political institutions, thereby raising the research question as to whether there is subordination of women in the guise of greater economic participation.

There is thus the necessity of examining the role and status of Manipuri women in the light of the global trend in both theory and empirics. The Sanakeithel of Manipur has been one most enduring institution reflecting these issues in relation to the women of the State. An appreciation of the position of women in this market would invariably enable us to understand the dynamics of women's status. This is done on the basis of responses to a structured questionnaire. While this has been a cross-sectional survey, the results gain much significance when situated in the light of data of different historical epochs. Three important pictures emerge from such an endeavour. First, the participation of women in outside-the-household activities continues to be still robust. Secondly, this participation cuts across the levels of academic qualification the women might possess. Thirdly, the institutional mechanism of this participation has always moved ahead of the times in the sense that the absence of supporting traditional or modern financial institutions has not deterred the continuation or expansion.

The historical strength of active participation of Manipuri women in society-wide issues still continues. It is as if the understanding of the important role that participation in outside the household economic activities can play in ameliorating living conditions has almost become generic to the women of Manipur, particularly so among the women vendors. This predominance of the economic factor can be both contextual as determined by the socio-economic situation of the society and personal as determined by the household level of wellbeing. A socio-politically more significant factor is the commitment of the women in the market to involve in organisations for collective cause as evident from the various historical movements for societal causes; this also could be a continuation of the inherent feature of the Manipuri women. This orientation for collective engagement for social responsibility gets reflected in the extra-ordinarily high level of participation in the electoral process. While more research is needed for understanding empowerment of the Manipuri women within the household decision-making process, their political-economic empowerment at the macro level is invariably seen.

In the course of the study, it came to light that certain related issues need further scrutiny while also at the same time taking up certain other issues not really related to the present study. In this section, we endeavour to identify some areas for further research.

First, it was seen that the sex ratio of Manipur became unfavourable to women from the 1961 Census but it bounced back after a gap of about four decades in the 2001 Census. A detailed examination of the micro-foundations of the dynamics of this short decline and recovery would have both theoretical and empirical values.

Secondly, whereas the pre-eminence of financial requirements as the reason for joining the labour market is evident overall, it becomes ambiguous when we examine the issue by family types. So, there is a need for a more detailed scrutiny of the dynamics of financial and non-financial pressure across types of family in Manipur.

Third, it was found that widows are joining the labour market predominantly because of economic pressure. This contrasts with the fairly high proportion of divorcees and married women joining the labour market in order to spend time. In order to strengthen this finding, it would be rewarding to examine the socio-economic dynamics of livelihood of women by different categories of marital status.

Fourthly, the economic empowerment of women in household decision-making comes out strongly from the results of the study. However, the low participation of women in non-economic areas of household decision-making appears to reduce the strength and depth of empowerment. So, the organisational dynamics of household decision-making would yield significant results when subjected to deeper scrutiny.

Fifth, a panel data study of the relative primacy of economic and psycho-social factors in determining the autonomy or otherwise of women in household decision-making is needed to give a clearer picture of the very decision-making process.

Sixth, given the spread and depth of economic empowerment of women, the impact of this on attitude and aptitude of women on world issues can be examined in order to draw global lessons for empowerment.

Lastly, another area of importance for study, though strictly not derived from the present study, would be an attempt to assess the health and nutritional status of the women vendors.

Bibliography

Ahluwalia, B. K., and Ahluwalia, S., (1984), ed., *Social Change in Manipur*, Cultural Publishing House, New Delhi.

Albanesi, S., and Olivetti, C., (2006), *Home Production, Market Production and the Gender Wage Gap: Incentives and Expectations*, NBER, Working Paper No. 12212.

_, (2007), *Gender Roles and Technological Progress*, NBER, Working Paper No. 13179.

Alderman, H. and Chisti, S., (1991), "Simultaneous Determination of Household and Market-Oriented Activities of Women in Rural Pakistan," *Research in Population Economics*, Vol. 7, pp. 245-265.

Allen, B.C., (1901), *Census of India, Vol. IV, Assam Part I*, Report, p. 162.

Altonji, J., and Blank, R., (1999), "Race and Gender in the Labor Market," in Ashenfelter, O., and Card, D., (1999), eds., *Handbook of Labor Economics*, Vol. 3, Amsterdam, North Holland.

Alsop, R., and A. Norton, (2004), "Power, Rights, and Poverty Reduction," in Alsop, R., (2005), ed., *Power, Rights, and Poverty: Concepts and Connections*, World Bank, Washington, D. C.

Alsop, R., Bertelsen, M., and Holland, J., (2006), *Empowerment in Practice: From Analysis to Implementation*, Poverty Reduction Group, World Bank, Washington, D.C.

Anxo, D., Flood, L., Mencarine, L., Pailhe, A., Solez, A., Letizia, M. Tanturri, (2007), "*Time Allocation between Work and Family over the Life-Cycle: A Comparative Gender Analysis of Italy, France, Sweden and the United States,*" IZA Discussion Paper No. 3193, November.

Appleton, S., Emwanu, T., Kagugube, J., and Muwonge, J., (1999), *Changes in Poverty in Uganda, 1992–1997*, Centre for the Study of African Economies, Oxford, U.K.

Arunachalam, J., and Kalpagam, U., (2007), ed., "*Rural Women in South Asia,*" Rawat Publications, Jaipur, India.

Asthana, S., (1996), "Women's Health and Women's Empowerment: A Locality Perspective," *Health and Place*, Vol. 2, No. 1, pp. 1–13.

Azad, N., (2007), "Towards an Engendered Poverty Paradigm in SAARC," in Arunachalam, J., and Kalpagam, U., (2007), ed., *Rural Women in South Asia*, Rawat Publications, Jaipur, p. 274.

Azfar, O., Kahkonen, S., and Meagher, P., (2001), *Conditions for Effective Decentralized Governance: A Synthesis of Research Findings*, Center for Institutional Reform and the Informal Sector, University of Maryland.

Bandasi, E., and Wodon, Q., (2009), *Working Long Hours and Having No Choice: Time Poverty in Guinea*, Gender Group, Poverty Reduction and Economic Management Network, Human Development Network, Development Dialogue on Values and Ethics, *Working Paper No. 4961*, World Bank, June.

Banerjee, N., (1999), "Women in the Emerging Labour Market," *The Indian Journal of Labour Economics*, Vol. 42, No. 4, pp.

Bardhan, K., (1985), "Women's Work, Welfare and Status Force of Tradition and Change in India," *Economic and Political Weekly*, Vol. XX, No. 50, Dec. 14.

Basu, A., and Basu, K., (1991), "Women's Economic Roles and Child Survival: the Case of India," *Health Transition Review*, Vol. 1, No. 1.

Becker, G., (1965), "A Theory of Allocation of Time," *Economic Journal*, Vol. 75, pp. 493-517.

Behrman, J., Foster, A., Rosenzweig, M., and Vashishtha, P., (1999), "Women's Schooling, Home Teaching, and Economic

Growth," *Journal of Political Economy*, Vol. 107, No. 4, pp. 683-713.

Beneria, L., and Bisnath, S., (1996), "Gender and Poverty: An Analysis for Action," *Gender in Development*, Monograph Series No. 2, UNDP.

Bernal, R., (2007), *The Effect of Maternal Employment and Child Care on Children's Cognitive Development*, Northwestern Working Paper.

Berry, B. L. J., (1967), *Geography of Market Centres and Retail Distribution*, Printice-Hall, New Jersey.

Besley, T., (2007), "The New Political Economy," *The Economic Journal*, pp. 570-587.

Bhadra, C., (2007), *International Labour Migration of Nepalese Women: Impact of their Remittances on Poverty Reduction*, Asia-Pacific Research and Training Network on Trade, Working Paper, Series No. 44.

Bhatt, E., (1989), "Toward Empowerment," *World Development*, Vol. 17, No.7, pp. 1059-1065.

Bhattacharya, M., Bedi, S. A., and Chhachhi, A., (2009), *Mariial Violence and Women's Employment and Property Status: Evidence from North Indian Villages*, IZA, Discussion Paper No. 4361.

Bianchi, S., (2000), "Maternal Employment and Time with Children: Dramatic Change or Surprising Continuity," *Demography*, Vol. 37, pp. 139-154.

Bisnath, Savitri and Elson, D., (1999), *Women's Empowerment Revisited*, Background paper, Progress of the World's Women, UNIFEM.Available: www.unifem.undp.org/progressww/empower.html.

Blackden, C. M., and Wodon, (2006), *Gender, Time Use and Poverty in Sub-Saharan Africa*, Working Paper No. 73, World Bank, Washington, D. C.

Blau, F. D., (1998), "Trends in the Wellbeing of American Women," *Journal of Economic Literature*, Vol. 36, No. 1, pp. 112-165.

Blau, F.D., and Kahn, L. M., (2003), "Understanding International Differences in the Gender Pay Gap," *Journal of Labor Economics*, Vol. 21, pp. 106-144.

Blau, F.D., and Lawrence, K., (2006), *Changes in the Labor Supply Behavior of Married Women: 1980-2000*, IZA Discussion Paper.

Blood and Wolfe, (1960), *Husbands and Wives: The Dynamics of Married Living*, The Free Press, New York.

Blumberg, R.L., (2005), *Women's Economic Empowerment as the Magic Potion of Development?*, Paper presented at the 100th Annual meeting of the American Sociological Association, Philadelphia.

Boserup, E., (1970), *Women's Role in Economic Development*, George Allen and Unwin, London.

Bossen, L., (1975), "Women in Modernizing Societies," *The American Ethnologist*, Vol.2.

Bowles, S., (1998), "Endogenous Preferences: The Cultural Consequences of Markets and Other Economic Institutions," *Journal of Economic Literature*, Vol. 36, No. 75, pp. 111.

Branisa, B., Klasen, S., Ziegler, M., (2009), *Why We Should All Care About Social Institutions Related To Gender Inequality*, Discussion Paper No. 15, Courant Research Centre, Gottingen University, October.

Brown, R., (1873), *Statistical Account of the Native State of Manipur, and the Hill Territory Under its Rule*, Reprinted in 2001, Mittal Publications, Delhi.

Burkhauser, Richard, V., Butler, J.S., and Holden, K.C. (1991), "How The Death of A Spouse Affects Economic Well-being After Retirement: A Hazard Model Approach," *Social Science Quarterly*, Vol. 72, No. 3, pp. 504-519.

Bourguignon, F., Ferreira, F., and Menendez, M., (2003), *Inequality of Outcomes and Inequality of Opportunities in Brazil*, Working Paper No. 3174, World Bank, Washington, D.C.

Calman, L.J. (1992), *Towards Empowerment: Women and*

Movement Politics in India, Westview Press, Boulder, Colorado.

Calvert, E., Russell, H., O'Connell, P., and McGinnity, F., (2009), *Reconciling Work and Family life: Workplaces, Occupation and the Experience of Work Life Conflict*, Economic and Social Research Institute, Research Bulletin 2009/3/4, Dublin, Ireland.

Carr, Marilyn, Chen, M., and Jhabvala, R., (1996), eds. "*Speaking Out: Women's Economic Empowerment in South Asia,*" IT Publications on behalf of Aga Khan Foundation Canada and UNIFEM, London.

Chattopadhyay, Raghabendra, and Duflo, E., (2001), *Women's Leadership and Policy Decisions: Evidence from a Nationwide Randomized Experiment in India,* IED Discussion Paper 114, Institute for Economic Development, Boston University.

Chaudhuri, S., (2010), *Women's Empowerment in South Asia and Southeast Asia: A Comparative Analysis*, MPRA Paper No. 19686.

Chen, N., Conconi, P., Peironi, P., (2007): *Women's Earning Power and Double Burden of Market and Household Work,* SOEP papers, German Institute for Economic Research, Berlin, p.1.

Claros, A.L., and Zahidi. S., (2005), *Women's Empowerment: Measuring the Global Gender Gap*, World Economic Forum, Geneva.

Coale, A.J., and Tye, C.Y. (1961), "The Significance of Age Patterns on Fertility in High Fertilising Population," *Milbank Memorial Fund Quarterly*, Vol.39, No. 4, pp. 631-646.

Constantine, R. (1981), *Manipur: Maid of the Mountains*, Lancers Publication, New Delhi.

Costa, D., (2000), "From Mill Town to Board Room: The Rise of Women's Paid Labor," *The Journal of Economic Perspectives*, Vol. 14, No.4, pp. 101-122.

Couto, R.A., (1998), "Community Coalitions and Grassroots Policies of Empowerment," *Administration and Society*, Vol. 30, No. 5, pp. 569–594.

Daron, A., and Robinson, J., (2006), *Economic Origins of Dictatorship and Democracy,* Cambridge University Press, New York.

Dena, L., (1991), ed., *History of Modern Manipur: 1826-1949,* Orient Publishers, New Delhi.

Dena, L., (2008), *British Policy Towards Manipur, 1762-1947,* Nongeen Publications, Manipur.

Deniz, K., (1990), "Women and Rural Development Policies-The Changing Agenda," *Development and Change,* Vol. 1, 21st January.

Desai, N., (1957), *Women in Modern India,* Vora Publishers, Bombay.

Desai, N., and Krishna Raj, (1987), *Women and Society in India,* Ajanta Publishers, Delhi.

Desai, N., and Thakkar, U., (2007), "Women and Political Participation in India," in *Women in Indian Society,* National Book Trust, New Delhi.

Devi, B. Ksh., (1988), "Manipuri Women – A Study," in Sanajaoba, N., (1988), *Manipur: Past and Present,* Mittal Publications, New Delhi.

Devi, L., (1982), *Status and Employment of Women in India,* B. R. Publishing Corporation, Delhi.

Devi, J., (1989), *Education in Manipur,* Rai Pravina Brothers, Imphal.

Devi, J., (1999), "Women's Movement in Manipur-Past and Present," in *Manipur Today,* DIPR, Government of Manipur, Imphal, 26th January, p.14.

Devicienti, F. and Poggi, A., (2007), *Poverty and Social Exclusion:Two Sides of the Same Coin or Dynamically Interrelated Processes?,* LABOR, Working Paper No. 62.

DFID, (2000), *Poverty Elimination and the Empowerment of Women: Strategies for Achieving the International Development Targets,* DFID, London.

Dianel, W., (1990), "Daughters, Decision and Domination," *Development and Change,* Vol. 21, No.1.

Dixon, R.B., (1978), *Rural Women at Work: Strategies for Development in South Asia,* John Hopkins University Press, Baltimore.

Diwan, R., (1995), Gender in Neo-Classical Economics, Conceptual Overview, *Economic and Political Weekly,* Vol. XXV, No. 17, April 29.

Dollar and Gatti, (1999), "Gender Inequality, Income and Growth: Are Good Times Good for Women?," *World Bank Policy Research Report on Gender and Development,* Working Paper No.1, World Bank, Washington, D.C.

Dollar, D., and Kraay, (2002), "Growth is Good for the Poor," *Journal of Economic Growth,"* Vol. 7, No. 3, pp. 195–225.

Duflo, E., (2003), "Grandmothers and Granddaughters: Old Age Pension and Intra-Household Allocation in South Africa," *World Bank Economic Review,* Vol. 42, pp. 1-25.

Dun, E.W., (1886), *Gazetteer of Manipur: compiled under the orders of the Quartermaster General in India,* Reprinted in 1975, Vivek Publishing House, Delhi.

Dyson, T., and Moore, M., (1983), "On Kinship Structure, Female Autonomy, and Demographic Behavior in India," *Population and Development Review,* Vol. 9, No. 1, pp. 35-60.

Elson, D., (1999), "Labor Markets as Gendered Institutions: Equality, Efficiency and Empowerment Issues," *World Development,* Vol. 27, No. 3, pp. 611-627.

Elson, D., and Pearson, R., (1997), "The Subordination of Women and the Internationalization of Factory Production," in Visvanathan, N., et al., (1997), eds., *The Women, Gender & Development Reader,* Zed Books, London.

Everett and Jana, (1991), *The Global Empowerment of Women,* Summary of the Annual Conference of the Association for Women in Development, November 17-19, 1989, Washington.

Eyben, R., (2003), *The Rise of Rights: Rights-Based Approaches to International Development,* Policy Briefing Issue 17, IDS, University of Sussex, Brighton, U.K.

Fafchamps, Marcel and Agnes, R. Quisimbing, (1998), *Social Roles, Human Capital and the Intra household Division of Labour: Evidence from Pakistan*, Department of Economics, Stanford University, Mimeograph.

Fisher, H., (1999), *The First Sex: The Natural Talents of Women and How They are Changing the World*, Random House, Inc, New York.

Fujita, M., Krugman, P., and Venables, A., (1999), *The Spatial Economy: Cities, Regions and International Trade*, Cambridge University Press, Cambridge.

Fujita, Masahisa and Tomoya Mori, (2005), Frontiers of the New Economic Geography, *Institute of Developing Economies, Discussion Paper No. 27*, April.

Galor, O., and Weil, D. N., (1996), "The Gender Gap, Fertility, and Growth," *American Economic Review, Vol.* 86, pp. 274-387.

Ganguly, J. B., (2006), *An Economic History of North East India, 1826 to 1947*, Akansha Publishing House, New Delhi.

Garnier, B. J., and Delobez, A., (1979), *Geography of Marketing*, Longman, London.

Gassah, L. S., (2008), *Women Empowerment Movement in North-East India*, Omsons Publications, New Delhi.

Gayle, G.L., and Golan, L., (2006), *Estimating a Dynamic Adverse Selection Model: Labor Force Experience and the Changing Gender Earnings Gap,* Carnegie Mellon Working Paper.

Goldin, C., (1990), *Understanding the Gender Gap: An Economic History of American Women,* Oxford University Press, New York.

Goldin, C., (2006), "The Quiet Revolution that Transformed Women's Employment, Education and Family," *American Economic Review,* Vol. 96, pp. 1-21.

Goodin, R., Rice, M. J., Parpo, A., and Eriksson, L., (2008), *Discretionary Time: A New Measure of Freedom*, Cambridge University Press, Cambridge.

Government of India, (1964), "International Trends," *Women in Employment*, Labour Bureau, Ministry of Labour and Employment, pp. 58-59.

Greenwood, J., Seshadri,A., and Yorugoklu, M., (2005), "Engines of Liberation," *The Review of Economic Studies*, Vol. 72, pp. 109-133.

Grimwood, E. St. C., (1891), *My Three Years in Manipur and Escape from the Recent Mutiny,* Reprinted in 1975, Vivek Publishing House, Delhi.

Gullason, E.T., (1999), "The Labor Market Status of Women," *Cato Journal*, Vol. 19, No. 1, pp. 101-118.

Gupta, M., (2000), ed., *Economic Participation of Women,* Vol.1, Sarup and Sons, New Delhi.

Haddad, Lawrence, and Hoddinott, J., (1994), "Women's Income and Boy-Girl Anthropometric Status in Cote d'Ivoire," *World Development,* Vol. 22, No. 4, pp. 543-553.

Hate, C.A., (1969), *Changing Status of Women in Post Independence India,* Allied Publication, Bombay, India.

Hashemi, S.M., Schuler, S. R., and Riley, A. P., (1996), "Rural Credit Programs and Women's Empowerment in Bangladesh," *World Development,* Vol. 24, pp. 635-653.

Heineck, G. (2004). "Does Religion Influence the Labour Supply of Married Women in Germany?," *Journal of Socio-economics,* Vol.33, No. 3, pp. 307-328.

Hochschild, A., (1989), *The Second Shift: Working Parents and the Revolution at Home,* Viking, New York.

Hodder, B. W., and Lee, R., (1974), *Economic Geography,* Metheun, London, p. 137.

Hoddinott, J., Adato, M., Besley, T., and Haddad, L., (2000), *Participation and Poverty Reduction: Issues, Theory and New Evidence from South Africa,* IFPRI,Washington,D.C. Available:http://www.worldbank.org/poverty/wdrpoverty/background/adatoetal.pdf.

Hoddinott, J., and Haddad, L., (1995), "Does Female Income Share

Influence Household Expenditures? Evidence from Cote d'Ivoire," *Oxford Bulletin of Economics and Statistics*, Vol. 57, No. 1, pp. 77-96.

Hodson, T.C., (1908), *The Meitheis—A Study of the Tribe of the Brahmaputra Valley*, Reprinted in 2010, Akansha Publishing House, New Delhi.

Ibungohal and Khelchandra, (1967), ed., *Cheitharol Kumbaba*, Manipuri Sahitya Parishad, Imphal.

Ilahi, N., (2001), "*Gender and the Allocation of Adult Time: Evidence from the Peru LSMS Panel Data*", The World Bank, Working Paper No. 2744.

Jain, D., (1985), *Women's Economic Roles and Women's Employment- The Linkages and Policy Implications*, Paper presented at the International Seminar on Women and Development, Jaipur, ISST.

Jain, D., (1996), *Panchayat Raj: Women Changing Governance*, United Nations Development Programme, New York. Available: http://www.undp.org/gender/resources/mono5.html

Jejeebhoy and Shireen, J., (2000), "*Women's Autonomy in Rural India: Its Dimensions, Determinants, and the Influence of Context*," in Presser, H., and Sen, G., eds., (2000), *Women's Empowerment and Demographic Processes: Moving Beyond Cairo*, Oxford University Press, New York.

Jejeebhoy, Shireen, J., and. Sathar, Z., (2001), "Women's Autonomy in India and Pakistan: The Influence of Religion and Region," *Population and Development Review*, Vol. 27, No. 4, pp. 687-712.

Jemol, U., (1990), "Work Participation of Women in India," *Economic and Political Weekly*, Vol. XXV, 10 March.

Johnstone, J., (1896), *My Experiences in Manipur and the Naga Hills*, Reprinted in 2002, Gyan Publishing House, New Delhi.

Jones, L.E., Manuelli, R.E., and Ellen R.M., (2003), *Why Are Married Women Working So Much*?, Federal Reserve Bank of Minneapolis Staff Report 317.

Joshi, S.C., (2004), *Women Empowerment: Myth and Reality*, Akansha Publishing House, New Delhi.

Kabeer, N., (1994), *Reversed Realities: Gender Hierarchies in Development Thought*, Verso, London.

Kabeer, N., (1999), *The Conditions and Consequences of Choice: Reflections on the Measurement of Women's Empowerment*, UNRISD Discussion Paper 108, Geneva.

Kabeer, N., (2001), "Resources, Agency, Achievements: Reflections on the Measurement of Women's Empowerment," in *Discussing Women's Empowerment—Theories and Practice, SIDA* Studies No. 3, Stockholm.

Kabeer, N., (2001), "Reflections on the Measurement of Women's Empowerment," in *Discussing Women's Empowerment-Theory and Practice*, SIDA Studies No. 3, Novum Grafiska AB, Stockholm.

Kabeer, N., (2001), "Conflicts over Credit: Re-evaluating the Empowerment Potential of Loans to Women in Rural Bangladesh," *World Development*, Vol. 29, pp. 63-84.

Kabeer, N., (2003), *Gender Mainstreaming in Poverty Eradication and the Millennium Development Goals*, Commonwealth Secretariat, London.

Kabeer and Mahmud, (2004), "Globalization, Gender and Poverty: Bangladesh Women Workers in Export and Local Market," *Journal of International Development*, Vol. 16, No. 1, pp. 93-109.

Kapur, P., (1970), *Marriage and the Working Women in India*, Vikas Publication, Delhi.

Karl, M., (1995), *Women and Empowerment: Participation and Decision-making*, Zed Books, London.

Kate, A., and Niels, G. (2008), "The Relevant Market: A Concept Still In Search Of A Definition," *Journal of Competition Law and Economics*, pp. 1-37, Oxford University Press, London.

Katz, L.F., Autor, D.H., (1999), "Changes in the Wage Structure and Earnings Inequality," in Ashenfelter, O., and Card, D., (1999), ed., *Handbook of Labor Economics*, pp. 1463-1555.

Kaufmann, D., Kraay, A., and Mastruzzi, M., (2004), "Governance Matters III: Governance Indicators for 1996–2002," *World Bank Economic Review,* Vol. 18, No. 2, pp. 253–287.

Khandker, Shahidur, R., (1988), "Determinants of Women's Time Allocation in Rural Bangladesh," *Economic Development and Cultural Change,* Vol. 37, pp. 111-126.

Khemani, R.S., and Shapiro, D.M., (1993), *Glossary of Industrial Organisation Economics and Competition Law,* commissioned by the Directorate for Financial, Fiscal and Enterprise Affairs, OECD.

King, E., and Evenson, E. Robert, (1983), "*Time Allocation and Home Production in Phillipine Rural Households,*" in Buvinic, M., Lycette, M.A., and McGreevey, W.P., (1983), eds., *Women and Poverty in the Third World,* Johns Hopkins University Press, Baltimore.

Klasen, S., (1999), *Does Gender Inequality Reduce Growth and Development? Evidence from Cross-Country Regressions,* PREM, Development Research Group, World Bank, Washington, D.C.Available: http://www.worldbank.org/gender/prr/wp7.pdf

Klein, V., (1965), *Britain Married Women Workers,* Routledge and Kegan Paul, London.

Kotler, P. and Zaltman, G. (1971), "Social Marketing: An Approach to Planned Social Change," *Journal of Marketing,* Chicago, Vol. 35, p. 5.

Krishnakumari, N.S., (1987), *Status of Single Women in India,* Uppal Publishing House, New Delhi.

Krishna Raj, M., (1978), *Report on Working Women Scientists in Bombay,* Research Unit of Women's Study, S.N.D.T. University, Bombay, India.

Krugman, P., (1991), "Increasing Returns and Economic Geography," *Journal of Political Economy,* Vol. 99, pp. 483-499.

Lokshin, M., and Ravallion, M., (2005), "Self-rated Power and Welfare in Russia," in Narayan, D., (2005), ed., *Measuring*

Empowerment: Cross-Disciplinary Perspectives, World Bank, Washington, D.C.

Lucas, R. (1988), "On the Mechanics of Economic Development," *Journal of Monetary Economics,* Vol-22, p. 3-42.

Lyall, A. in his introduction to Hodson, T.C., (1908), *The Meitheis*, David Nutt, London.

Lyngdoh, B., (2008), "Micro Finance and Women Empowerment: Some Evidences," *Man and Society-A Journal of North East Studies*, Vol. V, ICSSR, North Eastern Regional Centre, Shillong.

Majumder, V., (1978), *Status of Indian Women*, ICSSR, 1976.

Malhotra, M., (2004), *Empowerment of Women*, Vol-I, Isha Books, Delhi.

Malladi, S., (1985), *Women Tradition and Culture*, Sterling Publishers Private Limited, New Delhi.

Manipur Research Society, (2003), *Evolutionary Growth of the Khwairamband Keithel,* 7 September 2003.

Matthiassen, C. J., (1974), *Many Sisters-Women in Cross Cultural Perspective*, The Free Press, New York.

Mayoux, L., (2000), *Micro-finance and the Empowerment of Women: A Review of the Key Issues,* International Labor Organization, Geneva. Available:ilodata/public/english/ empoyment/finance/download/wp23.wpd

Medeiros, M., Guerreiro, R., Osorio, Costa, J., (2007), *Working Paper No. 34* "Gender Inequalities in Allocating Time to Paid and Unpaid Work: Evidence from Bolivia, International Poverty Centre,".

Mehra, R., (1997), "Women, Empowerment, and Economic Development," *The Annals of the Academy,* Vol. 554, pp. 136-149.

Mehrotra, D.P., (2009), *Burning Bright: Irom Sharmila and the Struggle for Peace in Manipur*, Penguin Books, India.

Mies, M., (1980), *Indian Women and Patriarchy: Conflicts and Dilemmas of Students and Working Women*, Concept Publishing House, New Delhi.

Moore, M., and Putzel, J., (1999), *Thinking Strategically about Politics and Poverty,* IDS, Working Paper No. 101, University of Sussex, Brighton, U.K.

Morgan, D. H. J., (1975), *Social Theory and the Family,* Routledge and Kegan Paul, London.

Morrison, Andrew, and Lamana, F., (2006), *Gender Issues in the Kyrgyz Labour Market,* Background paper for Kyrgyz Poverty Assessment, World Bank, Washington, D.C.

Morrison, A., Raju, D., Sinha, D., (2007), *Gender Equality, Poverty and Economic Growth,* PREM, Working Paper No. 4349.

Moser, C., and Norton, A., (2001), *To Claim Our Rights: Livelihood Security, Human Rights, and Sustainable Development,* Overseas Development Institute, London.

Mujeri, M.K., (2002), *Gender Issues at the Local Level: Summary Results of a Pilot Survey in Bangladesh,* Working Paper No. 11, under MIMAP Project, Bangladesh.

Mukerji, S.N., (1961), *History of Education in India,* Acharya Books, Baroda.

Mukhyopadhyay, S., (1999), *Women's Work in South Asia: A Situational Analysis and Policy Concerns,* SAAT, New Delhi.

Mukhyopashyay, S., and Sudarshan, R. M., (2003), eds., *Tracking Gender Equity Under Economic Reforms: Continuity and Change in South Asia,* IDRC and Kali for Women, New Delhi.

Mullan, C.S., (1932), *Census of India, 1931-Vol. III-Assam-Part I,* Report, Shillong.

Mulvihill, D.F., and Mulvihill, R.L., (1970), *Geography, Marketing and Urban Growth,* Van Nostrand.

Murduck, (1949), *Our Primitive Contemporaries,* The Macmillan Company, New York.

Murduck and Leistritz, (1988), *The Farm Financial Crisis,* Boulder Westview Press.

Murthi, R.K. (1984), "Daring Dames of Manipur," in Ahluwalia, B.K., and Ahluwalia, S., (1984), *op. cit.,* p. 73.

Myrdal, Alva and Viola Klein, (1962), *Women's Two Roles*, Routledge and Kegan Paul, London.

Naik, J. P., and Syed, N., (1974), *A Students History of Education in India (1800-1973)*, Macmillan, Bombay.

Narayan, D., et. al., (2002), *Empowerment and Poverty Reduction*, PREM, World Bank, Washington, D. C.

Narayan, D., and Shah, T., (2000), *Gender Inequity, Poverty & Social Capital*, PREM, WorldBank, Washington, D. C.

Narayan,D. and Shah, T., (2000), *Connecting the Local to the Global: Voices of the Poor*, World Bank, Washington, D.C.

Narayan, D., Patel, R., Schafft, K., Rademacher, A., and Koch-Schulte, S., (2000), *Voices of the Poor: Can Anyone Hear Us?*, Oxford University Press, New York.

Nayak, P., and Mahanta, B., (2009), *Women Empowerment in India*, MPRA Paper No. 12685.

North, D., (1990), *Institutions, Institutional Change and Economic Performance: Political Economy of Institutions and Decisions*, Cambridge University Press, Cambridge.

North, D., Wallis, J., and Weingast, B., (2006), *A Conceptual Framework for Interpreting Recorded Human History*, Working Paper No. 12795, NBER, December.

Nussbaum, M., (1999), *Sex and Social Justice*, Oxford University Press, New York.

Nussbaum, M., (2000), *Women and Human Development: The Capabilities Approach*, Cambridge Press, New York.

Nieva, F., and Gutek, B., (1981), *Women and Work: A Psychological Perspective*, Praeger Publishers, New York.

Olivetti, C., and Petrongolo, B., (2006), *Unequal Pay or Unequal Employment? A Cross-country Analysis of Gender Gaps*, CEPR Discussion Paper 5506.

Ottaviano, Gianmarco I.P., and Jacques-Francois, T., (2004), *New Economic Geography: What About the N?*, Mimeo., September.

Pandhya, R., (2008), ed., *Women Welfare and Empowerment in India-Vision for 21st Century,* New Century Publications, New Delhi.

Pandolfelli, L., Meinzen-Dick, R., and Dohrn, S., (2007), Gender and Collective Action: A Conceptual Framework for Analysis, Paper presented at the International Research Workshop on '*Gender and Collective Action*' October, 17-21, 2005, Chiang Mai, Thailand, CAPRi, Working Paper No. 64, IFPRI.

Pirenne, H., (1936), *Economic and Social History of Medieval Europe*, New York.

Polanyi, K., (1957), *Trade and Markets in Early Empires*, Glencoe.

Potts, M., Hayden, T., (2008), *Sex and War: How Biology Explains Warfare and Terrorism and Offers a Path to a Safer World,* Benbella Books, Dallas.

Pryor, F. L., (2007), "Culture and Economic Systems,"*American Journal of Economics and Sociology,* Vol. 66, No. 4, pp. 818-855.

Rahman, L., and Rao, V., (2004), "The Determinants of Gender Equity in India: Examining Dyson and Moore's Thesis with New Data," *Population and Development Review*, Vol. 30, No. 2, pp. 239-268.

Ramanamma, (1979), *Graduate Employed Women in an Urban Setting*, Dastane Ramachandra and Company, Poona, India.

Ranade, S. N., and Ramachandran, P., (1970), *Women and Employment: Reports of Pilot Studies conducted in Delhi and Bombay,* Tata Institute of Social Sciences, Bombay, India.

Ravallion, (2001), *Growth, Inequality and Poverty: Looking Beyond Average,* Development Research Group, World Bank, Washington, D.C.

Ravallion, M., and Chen, S., (2001), *Measuring Pro-poor Growth*, Policy Research Working Paper No. 2666, World Bank, Washington.

Rodríguez, F. (2008), *What Makes Growth Shared? On the Political Economy of Inclusive Development*, Paper presented at the Annual Bank Conference on Development Economics, South Africa.

Ross, A., (1961), *Hindu Family in an Urban Setting*, Oxford University Press, New York.

Rozario, S., (2002), "Gender Dimensions of Rural Change," in Toufique, K.A., and Turton, C., (2002), eds., *Hands Not Land: How Livelihood are Changing in Rural Bangladesh*, Bangladesh Institute of Development Studies, University of Sussex, UK.

Ruhm, C., (2004), "Parental Employment and Child Cognitive Development," *Journal of Human Resources,* Vol. 39, No. 1, pp. 155-192.

Saikia, P.D., (1980), *Indian Rural Women's*, Mittal Publications, Delhi.

Sanajaoba, N., (1988), *Manipur: Past and Present*, Mittal Publications, Delhi.

Sandell, S., and Howard, I., (1997), "Reducing Women's Poverty by Shifting Social Security Benefits from Retired Couples to Widows," *Journal of Policy Analysis and Management,* Vol. 16, No. 2, pp. 279-297.

Sathar, Z., and Kazi, S., (1997), *Women's Autonomy, Livelihood and Fertility: A Case of Rural Punjab*, PIDE, Islamabad.

Saxena, H.M, (1984), *Geography of Marketing*, Sterling, New Delhi.

Saxena, H.M., (1988), *Chapter II, Rural Markets and Development*, Rawat Publication, Jaipur.

Scanjoni, M., (1980), *Family Decision Making: A Developmental Sex Role Model*, Sage Publications, London.

Schmid, G. (1984), *Sex Discrimination and Equal Opportunity: The Labor Market and Employment Policy*, Palgrave Macmillan.

Schuler, S.R. and Hashemi, S.M. (1994), "Credit Programs, Women's Empowerment, and Contraceptive Use in Rural Bangladesh," *Studies in Family Planning,* Vol. 25, No. 2, pp. 65-76.

Schumpeter, J., (1961), *The Theory of Economic Development:*

An Inquiry into Profits, Capital, Credit, Interest and the Business Cycle, Oxford University Press, New York.

Sen, A., (1985), "Well-being, Agency and Freedom, The Dewey Lectures 1984," *The Journal of Philosophy*, Vol. 82, No. 4, pp. 169-221.

Sen, A., (1997), "Editorial: Human Capital and Human Capability," *World Development*, Vol.25, No. 12, pp. 1959–1961.

Sen, A., (1999), *Development as Freedom*, Oxford University Press, *New York*.

Sen, G., and Caren, G., (1987), *Development, Crises, and Alternative Visions: Third World Women's Perspectives*, Monthly Review Press, New York.

Sesodia, J.S., (1985), "Role of Women in Agriculture: A Study of Chambal Command of Madhya Pradesh," *Indian Journal of Agriculture Economics*, Vol. 40.

Shah, S. (2006), "Sexual Division of Labour in Adam Smith's Work," *Journal of the History of Economic Thought*, Vol. 28, pp. 221-241.

Shakespear, J., (1907), *Manipur under British Management* 1891-1907, Shillong.

Sharma, H. Dwijasekhar (2009), ed., *New Insights into the Glorious Heritage of Manipur*, Vol. 3, Akansha Publishing House, New Delhi.

Sharma, U., (1983), *Women's Work and Property in North-West India*, Tavistock Publications, London.

Simon, J. (1981), *The Ultimate Resource*, Princeton University Press, Princeton.

Sinclair, J., (1996), "Women and Technology, Problem of Technological Unemployment or De Skillings," *Economic and Political Weekly*, Vol. XXXI, No.16 and No. 17, April 20-27.

Singh, I.N., (2003), *The Manipur Administration, (1709-1907)*, Horizon Printers, New Delhi.

Singh, K.P., (1988), *Women and Development*, National Seminar, The Emerging Perspective of India's Development Experience,

Chandigarh, March 10-12.

Singh, L.J., (1995), *The Lost Kingdom*, Prajatantra Publishing House, Imphal.

Singh, N.J., (1991), "*Anti-British Movement: 1904-1949,*" in Dena, L., ed., (1991), *History of Modern Manipur: 1826-1949*, Orient Publishers, New Delhi, pp. 122-123.

Singh and Singh, (1987), "Impact of Rural Development on Economics-Status of Women in Uttar Pradesh," *Kurukshetra*, Vol. XXXV, No. 8.

Sircar, M. Chaki, (1984), *Feminism in a Traditional Society: Women of Manipur Valley*, Vikas Publishing House, Delhi.

Standing, H., (1985), "Resources, Wages, and Power: the Impact of Women's Employment on the Urban Bengali Household," in Afshar, H., (1985), ed., *Women, Work, and Ideology in the Third World*, Tavistock Publications, New York.

Stern, N., (2001), *A Strategy for Development*, World Bank, Washington, D.C.

Stern, N., (2002), *Gender and Human Development,* Oxford University Press, U.K.

Stern, N., Dethier, J., and Rogers, H., (2005), *Growth and Empowerment: Making Development Happen*, MIT Press, Cambridge.

Tzannatos, Z., (1999), "Women and Labour Market Changes in the Global Economy: Growth Helps, Inequalities Hurt and Public Policy Matters," *World Development*, Vol. 27, No. 3, pp. 551-569.

Thomas, D., (1990), "Intrahousehold Resource Allocation: An Inferential Approach," *Journal of Human Resources, Vol.* 25, pp. 635-664.

Thomas, D., (1997), "Incomes, Expenditures, and Health Outcomes: Evidence on Intrahousehold Resource Allocation," in Haddad, L., Hoddinott, J., and Alderman, H., eds. (1997), *Intrahousehold Resource Allocation in Developing Countries: Models, Methods, and Policy*, Johns Hopkins University Press, Baltimore.

United Nations (1996), *Report of the Fourth World Conference on Women: Beijing, 4-15 September 1995*, New York.

United Nations Development Programme (UNDP), (1995), *Human Development Report 1995: Gender and Human Development*, Oxford University Press, New York.

United Nations Development Programme (UNDP), (1998), *Human Development Report 1998: Consumption for Human Development*, Oxford University Press, New York.

United Nations Division for the Advancement of Women (UNDAW), (2001), *Empowerment of Women Throughout the Life Cycle as a Transformative Strategy for Poverty Eradication,* Department of Economic and Social Affairs, Report of the Expert Group Meeting, 26-29 November, New Delhi.

Vaghaiwalla, R.B., (1951), *Census of India,* Volume XII, Assam, Manipur and Tripura, Part I-A, Report, p. 39.

Varshney, (2005), "*Democracy and Poverty*" in *Measuring Empowerment: Cross-Disciplinary Perspectives,* World Bank, Washington, D. C.

Wanmali, S., (1981), *Periodic Markets and Rural Development in India,* B. R. Publishing Corporation, Delhi.

Weissberg, R., (2000), "The Vagaries of Empowerment," *Society,* Vol. 37, No. 2, pp. 15–21.

Whitman,P., (1997), Chapter 3,"Religion and Women's Human Rights," in Whitman,P., (1997), ed., *Religion and Contemporary Liberalism*, University of Notre Dame Press, Notre Dame, pp. 93-137.

Wodon, Q., (1997), "Food Energy Intake and Cost of Basic Needs: Measuring Poverty in Bangladesh," *Journal of Development Studies,* Vol. 34, pp. 66–101.

World Bank, (2001a), *Engendering Development: Through Gender Equality in Rights, Resources, and Voice,* World Bank Policy Research Report, Oxford University Press, New York.

World Bank, (2001b), *World Development Report 2001: Attacking Poverty*, Oxford University, Press New York.

World Bank, (2000c), *World Development Report 2000/2001: Attacking Poverty,* Oxford University Press, New York. Available:http://www.worldbank.org/poverty/wdrpoverty/report/index.html.

World Bank (2008), *World Development Indicators,* available at http://www.globalissues.org/article/26/poverty-facts-and-stats

World Economic Forum, (2009), *Global Gender Gap Report 2009,* Geneva.

World Economic Forum, (2009), *The India Gender Gap Review 2009,* Geneva.

Wodon, Q., (1997), "Food Energy Intake and Cost of Basic Needs: Measuring Poverty in Bangladesh." *Journal of Development Studies,* Vol. 34, pp. 66–101.

Wodon, (1999), *Growth, Inequality, and Poverty: A Regional Panel for Bangladesh,* Policy Research Working Paper 2072, World Bank, Washington, D.C.

Wodon, (2000), *Public Works Employment and Workfare Programs: Optimizing the Timing of Benefits for Poverty Reduction,* PREM, World Bank, Washington, D.C.

Yale, S., (1989), "The Status of Women in India," Review Article, *Pacific Affairs,* Vol.62, No.3.

Yumnam, A., (1996), *Economics of Feminism: A Selective Survey,* Omeo Kumar Das, Institute of Social Change and Development, Guwahati.

Yumnam, A., (2005), "Development Experience of Manipur: A Framework for Industrialization," in Das, G., (2005), ed., *Structural Change and Strategy of Development, Resource-Industry Linkages in North-East India,* Akansha Publishing House, New Delhi, p. 83.

Yumnam, A., (2009), North East: Time To Move from Nash Equilibrium to Specialist Equilibrium, Presidential Address delivered at the 11th Annual Conference of the North Eastern Economic Association held at the Indian Institute of Technology, Guwahati, December.

Zaman, H., (1999), *Assessing the Poverty and Vulnerability Impact of Micro-Credit in Bangladesh: A Case Study of BRAC,* World Bank, Washington, D. C.

Websites Consulted:

1. www.google.com
2. www.nber.org
3. www.worldbank.org
4. www.undp.org
5. www.worldbank.org
6. www.globalissues.org
7. www.ilodata.org

Index

***